. . . LIFELINES . . .

Survival Tips for Parents of Preschoolers

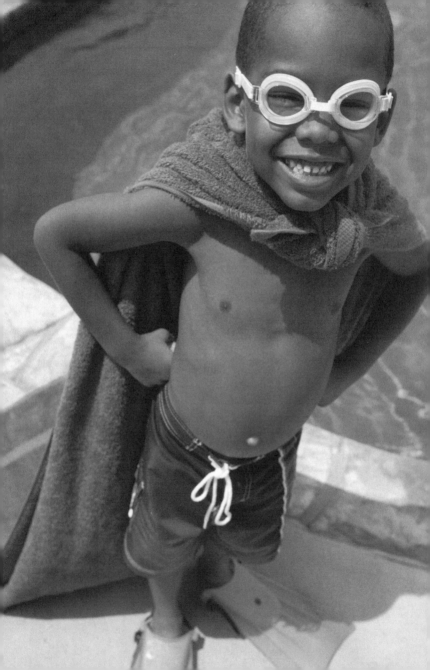

...LIFELINES...

SURVIVAL TIPS

FOR PARENTS OF

PRESCHOOLERS

BECKY FREEMAN

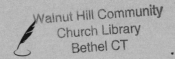

Walnut Hill Community
Church Library
Bethel CT

Tyndale House Publishers, Inc.
WHEATON, ILLINOIS

F m
6 49.12
Fre

Visit Tyndale's exciting Web site at www.tyndale.com

Designed by Ron Kaufmann

Published in association with the literary agency of Alive Communications, Inc., 7680 Goddard Street, Suite 200, Colorado Springs, CO 80920.

Library of Congress Cataloging-in-Publication Data

Freeman, Becky, date.
  Survival tips for parents of preschoolers / Becky Freeman.
    p. cm. — (Life lines)
Includes bibliographical references.
  ISBN 0-8423-6018-2 (pbk.)
  1. Child rearing. 2. Parenting. 3. Preschool children. 4. Child rearing—religious aspects—Christianity. 5. Parenting—Religious aspects—Christianity. I. Title. II. Series.
HQ769.F728 2003
649'.123—dc21   2002152202

Printed in the United States of America

07 06 05 04 03
7   6   5   4   3   2   1

. . . ABOUT LIFE LINES . . .

The Life Lines series is designed for *real* people in *real life* situations. Written by published authors who are experts in their field, each book covers a different topic and includes:

- information you need, in a quick and easy-to-read format
- practical advice and encouragement from someone who's been there
- "life support"—hands-on tips to give you immediate help for the problems you're facing
- "healthy habits"—long-term strategies that will enrich your life
- inspiring Bible verses
- lists of additional resources—books, Web sites, videos, and seminars to keep you headed on the right path

Life Lines is a joint effort from Marriage Alive International and Smalley Relationship Center. Marriage Alive founders and directors David and Claudia Arp serve as general editors.

Whether you need assistance for an everyday situation, a life transition, or a crisis period, or you're just looking for a friend to come alongside you, Life Lines offers wise, compassionate counsel from someone who can help. This series will connect with you, inspire you, and give you tools that will change your life—for the better!

Titles in the series:
Life Lines: Connecting with Your Husband—Gary Smalley
Life Lines: Connecting with Your Wife—Barbara Rosberg

To all those peanut-butter-covered moms,
who are sacrificing manicures
and a full night's sleep to do the most
difficult and important job on the planet:
to love and raise small children.
I salute you!
Becky

. . . CONTENTS . . .

Do you ever wonder . . .

- how "sleeping in" came to mean actually making it until the late hour of 7:00 A.M. before being awakened by the *pitter-patter* of noisy preschooler feet?
- what happened to the days when you could sit down and read a whole magazine article or a one-page devotional without being interrupted six times?
- if you'll ever again be able to take a ten-minute shower without a small visitor entering the bathroom?
- when you'll get dressed for church in an ensemble that doesn't include jelly smears and Barney Band-Aids?
- when you'll be able to walk through your house barefoot in the dark without stepping on Legos or those tiny Barbies?

Your life has never been the same since you brought that new baby into your house, and the challenges just keep coming. If your little bundle of adventure is now a fast-moving, curious, talkative two-, three-, or four-year-old, you're at the peak period of parent frustration. These are the days when you can't blink without opening your eyes to find your little one climbing the garden trellis or experimenting with permanent markers. These are the days when you can't finish a cup of coffee—or an entire thought—without your little one requiring your attention to approve his latest daring feat or to kiss her most recent boo-boo. These are the days when Mommy and Daddy's fund of ideas for worthwhile pastimes runs far shorter than their preschooler's energy and desire for more!

But even when you run out of steam—and ideas— by 11:30 A.M., you want what's best for your preschool-aged child—and it costs you. It costs your time, attention, creativity, and energy—when sometimes there are other priorities battling for that same time, attention, creativity, and energy. If ever there was a stage that felt like an unstoppable merry-go-round, these preschool years are that stage.

So what's a parent to do? Get all the help you can— help for making that carousel ride enjoyable while it lasts, and help for stopping it once in a while so both you and your little one can rest.

HELP IS ON THE WAY

If you find yourself at the end of your rope, questioning how to handle the latest tantrum or wondering if there are any steps you can take to retain your sanity, this book is for you! Whether you stay at home with your children, work at home, or juggle parenting with a job outside the home, you face similar frustrations and challenges. I want to help! So I'm mustering all the strength of my experience and education in order to bring you encouragement and advice.

After all, I am a fellow survivor! Together with my husband, I have managed to live to tell about the ten years we spent raising four preschoolers. Believe it or not, I managed to take careful notes during those years so that I would never forget the love, laughter, and exhaustion of being a mommy to small children (a full-time job whether or not you also work outside the home). I remember those years like the back of a chubby little peanut-butter-and-jelly-covered hand.

> If ever there was a stage that felt like an unstoppable merry-go-round, these preschool years are that stage.

After a ten-year mommy break, I went back to college and completed my degree in elementary and early childhood education. I then taught little ones in public school for a short time—okay, a *very* short time. After a mere nine months of faithful service, I was able to make writing from home a paying proposition and felt glad to get back with my own children during the day.

For this book, I've gathered knowledge about what

. . .

really works from my own experience, and I've also researched and combed through the best parenting books. I've explored child psychology and visited with two kinds of experts. Some were professionals with Ph.D.'s in early childhood; some were fellow parents who could pass on creative suggestions.

So here it is in a nutshell: the best help for parents of preschoolers. Because let's face it, right now you probably do not have time to go to the bathroom alone, much less read through an extensive *Encyclopedia of Proper Parenting*. You could call this a bit of life support for you, the parent.

In these pages, we'll look at two main areas. First, how can you take care of yourself so you'll be a better, less irritable, and more rested parent? We'll look at some "life support" ideas—things you can do immediately to lighten your load—as well as some healthy habits you can develop that will enrich your life in the long run.

Second, we'll look at some of the main dilemmas facing parents of preschoolers and offer some problem-solving ideas. We'll talk about how preschoolers operate, and then we'll touch on potty training, finicky eaters, temper tantrums, and bedtime. I'll give you some tips on how to fill your day with worthwhile pastimes—for both you and your child. Hang on—help is on the way.

．　．　．

   I'm happy to report that every last one of our pre-schoolers is now a happy, functioning teenager or adult—not that there weren't, as there continue to be, some amazing ups and downs on their way to young adulthood. But we made it—both parents and children! And so will you.

A DAY IN THE LIFE

Here's a typical day in the life of a stay-at-home parent of a preschooler:

6:43 A.M. She's awakened with the gentle tap-tap-tapping of a small sticky hand on her sleep-laden eyelids. Gingerly, she opens one eye. Though the scene is a little fuzzy (jelly in the eyelashes doesn't help), she can make out one preschooler in sleeper pajamas holding a jar of grape jelly to his chest with his left hand, patting her tenderly with the other dimpled, jelly-coated right hand.

She smiles weakly as this child asks her to help him find the peanut butter.

7:56 A.M. Having inhaled a cup of coffee, she is now standing at the mirror, bearing only a vague resemblance to her former before-kids self, removing grape jelly pats from various and sundry parts of her body.

Preschooler is wailing in the time-out chair, where he's been banished for throwing a rabidlike fit when his peanut butter and jelly toast was cut diagonally instead of up and down. She estimates the remainder of his three-minute time-out, wondering if it's safe to risk taking the world's fastest speed-bath—alone. She sighs wistfully for those halcyon days when drawing a hot bubble bath signaled anticipated time alone, not an invitation to a hot-tub party for little people.

> The challenges of parenting are intense—and unrelenting.

11:07 A.M. She opens cupboards and drawers and dumps out the toy box while looking, in vain, for a pound of hamburger she was sure was thawing on the kitchen counter. When she checks on the preschooler playing in the sandbox outside, she's just in time to see him holding the pound of hamburger by one end, giggling as the kitty happily gorges herself on the unexpected treat.

1:14 P.M. She reads *Pat the Bunny* six times, until finally, blessedly, the little fellow falls asleep. Tiptoeing out of the room, she glances back at the child's long lashes, his little round tummy rising and falling with each breath, and dashes back to kiss his soft cheek. Then she tosses the mental coin: Does she take a nap or clean the house that looks as if it's falling down around her ears? She yawns and sinks down beside the resting child, curling her body around his, sucked into the undertow of sleep.

3:22 P.M. On a walk to the park she answers seventy-six questions, all beginning with "Why," "What," or "How." She is a walking encyclopedia of preschooler knowledge: why some worms wear sweaters, why fingers have two elbows, what baby robins eat. Forget *Who Wants to Be a Millionaire?* If they only had a game show called *Who Wants to Be a Mommy?* she'd win—and big. Keeping a preschooler informed—with age-appropriate answers—takes more stamina and more scientific knowledge than any existing game show, and it requires gargantuan nerves of steel.

5:00 P.M. She makes a stab at a slapdash job of housekeeping and opens a can of SpaghettiOs for dinner (since little Prince Charming made sure Kitty enjoyed tonight's originally planned entree). She hears an ear-shattering clatter—an all-too-familiar noise she's come to dread. The offspring has managed to pull the toy box into the kitchen and dump the contents on the tile floor—again. She wonders how he gets the strength to haul a huge toy box from room to room, but goes weak-kneed and limp when required to pick up one plastic Duplo block.

6:53 P.M. Dad comes through the door and surveys the daily damage that a three-foot child can wreak upon a two-thousand-square-foot house. He looks hopefully toward the kitchen stove, frowns, and asks, "So tell me, what did you do all day?"

9:47 P.M. The little one is finally asleep after a thirty-minute wild romp in the bathtub (splashing enough water on the floor to float a battleship), ten more readings of *Pat the Bunny*, six choruses of "I want a drink of water," and four of "I need to go potty." She stumbles to her own room, notices a hopeful look on her husband's face and silently turns the small decorative pillow face up, so that the "Definitely Not Tonight" embroidered message can say it all. He pouts. She reminds him that the "What did you do all day?" question didn't exactly get her love motor in gear.

10:14 P.M. She falls asleep while trying to remember the calm, collected, organized woman she was before stretch marks, spit-up, and tantrums rocked her world. Her husband lies in the dark, fondly remembering when "teddies" meant sexy lingerie instead of stuffed fuzzy bears.

That's a basic agenda for a parent who's home all day. The parent who works part-time or full-time has to come up with pants with no orange-juice stains, a briefcase without oatmeal dumped inside, and time to do three loads of laundry between the preschooler's bedtime and her own. The working parent puts in long hours of dealing with work pressures and people and comes home longing for a haven of rest and refreshment—only to find that Junior still has plenty of energy and wants to use it all playing with Mom or Dad. The challenges of parenting are intense—and unrelenting.

> Any mom or dad still standing and smiling at the end of a typical week home alone with small children deserves a medal of honor.

Even though you and your spouse both love your child more than life itself, do you ever wonder if you actually have the strength to raise him without losing your mind (or your marriage)?

If this mom's scenario seemed awfully familiar, no doubt it's because your own days are riddled with the unexpected from the moment you wake up until you drop into bed at night. Whatever plans you make are subject to change completely, depending on the moods and mishaps your preschooler brings to the mix. That combination of reasoned, intentional planning and rolling-with-whatever-comes is hard to achieve with grace—and with your temper under control.

I have a sincere empathy for men and women in this stage of parenting. These preschool years—before a child moves on to more independent pastimes and an ability to go fifteen minutes without Mom's or Dad's attention—are especially tough. When I'm asked in interviews which stage of parenting I consider the most difficult, I don't hesitate to name the preschool years. Though teenagers bring their own set of challenges, the most physically and mentally demanding and exhausting stage of parenting is the time when your children are preschoolers. There are so few "breathers" for the parent of a preschooler, whose neediness is nonstop. For a few years, you can't let your guard down ("It's too quiet. What are they up to now?"), can't go take a nap anytime you want (and you want one all the time), can't take your eyes off them ("Where did they go?"), can't go to the bathroom alone *(Knock, knock, knock.* "Mommy, can I come in? What are you doing, Mommy?" *Knock, knock, knock)*.

In researching the most prevalent problems parents of preschoolers face, I found that exhaustion and burnout top the list. Feelings of isolation (for

. . .

both stay-at-home parents and working parents who are too busy for their friends) and aching spiritual needs run a close second.

Parents of preschoolers are looking for information, asking almost as many questions as their little ones:

- How can I get some rest and stay healthy?
- How early is too early to potty train?
- How can I get her to eat?
- What do I do when he throws a tantrum?
- I get so much advice, but which child-rearing technique really is best?
- How do I keep my child occupied without resorting to too much TV?
- If I'm home all day with the kids, how can I keep my brain from atrophying?
- What will make bedtime easier for the whole family?
- How can I teach my child about God?

In these pages, we'll touch on all of these areas and more.

If we put a childless, well-dressed CEO of a major corporation into a home with two or three preschoolers (ah, toss in a baby, too, just for fun) and evaluated the CEO at the end of the week, I guarantee that he would no longer be the same person—physically or mentally. In fact, my guess is that the CEO would be on his knees, begging to be allowed to go back to work.

Parents don't have an easy out, and deep down they don't really want one. This God-given child is theirs to love and discipline—to shape for a healthy, productive grown-up life. After all, Proverbs 22:6 tells us, "Teach your children to choose the right path, and when they are older, they will remain upon it." Because they love their children, parents hang in there. I personally feel that any mom or dad who is still standing and smiling at the end of a typical week home alone with small children deserves a medal of honor.

Want to earn that medal of honor? This book holds some of the keys of help and humor to get you to the end of each day.

2

LIFE SUPPORT: NAP TIME FOR MOM AND DAD

Let's say one day as I sit typing this book in delicious peace (considering that all my nearly-grown children are tucked away at school, college, or work), there comes a knock at my front door.

I stroll to open it—and gasp at the sight. There on the porch stands an obviously frazzled woman at the end of her mental rope. Her eyes are red-rimmed with tears and sleep deprivation, the hem of her denim skirt has the telltale signs of small yogurt handprints, and there are two round wet spots on her blouse (indicating the overflow of a nursing mother). In hands that have not seen a manicure in months, she clutches a small red suitcase. (It says "Going to Grandma's" in

• • •

bright, cartoon letters.) There's a cardboard sign around her neck (dangling from a necklace made with yarn and Froot Loops), which has hand-scrawled letters reading, "Will Beg for One Hour's Peace." Weakly, she manages to say, "I'm a mother of small children and frankly, I just can't take it anymore. I'm running away from home! Can you help me?"

"Say no more," I tell her soothingly, reaching out to pull her into my arms, then into my kitchen for a hot cup of tea. In this house, she can get tea without a single cracker crumb or Cocoa Puff floating on the top!

This mother doesn't need a lecture on child psychology; she doesn't need a 365-page parenting manual. She needs a nap. She needs some love. She needs some encouragement and refreshment. Only after her most immediate needs are tended to will we be able to move on to practical ways to help her love, nurture, and discipline her children.

Just as the flight attendant always tells parents to put on their own oxygen masks before helping their children with theirs, the first step in helping parents to be of real help to their children is to nurture the nurturer.

So even though you may not be out on the street looking like you've been hit by a Mack truck (yet), you probably know the feeling of longing for some rest, some personal attention, some TLC just for you.

. . .

So let's tend to first things first and get Mom and Dad some immediate relief and refreshment. Think of this as your own personal pep talk and hug from one parent in the trenches to another.

THE ABSOLUTE MUST OF REST

Dr. James B. Maas, professor of a hugely popular "sleep course" at Cornell University and author of the best-selling book *Power Sleep,* writes, "A parent of a new baby loses 400 to 750 hours of sleep during the first year. Approximately 30 percent of young children (one to four years old) demand parental intervention at least once nightly."[1] Whoa! No wonder you can't concentrate!

Sleep deprivation can turn any human being into a zombie, making small irritations seem enormous and affecting your ability to perceive and communicate. In other words, without sufficient sleep, you'll turn yourself into a big cranky toddler in need of a nap. And the last thing your home needs right now is one more little person!

But you already know you need some rest; you don't need me to convince you. How will you get it? Unless you're a single parent, there's another adult in your family. So start on the road to rest by working out a deal with your spouse. A lot of children—especially those who have been up during the night—are

. . .

actually good morning sleepers. So if you've been getting up early to see your spouse off in the morning, talk to him or her about exchanging your morning attention for some bedtime attention. Most men, I know, will happily forgo a hot breakfast in the morning in trade for a hot mama in the evening!

Scientists have proven that our most creative times of day are just before drifting to sleep and when we wake up.

I, for one, have *never* been a morning person. And even though our kids are teenagers now, my husband, the early riser, gets up with them, hangs out with them over eggs or breakfast cereal, and then brings me coffee in bed! I love this arrangement. In exchange, he gets the luxury treatment when he comes home from work. At that time of day, I'm fully functional and can help the kids with their homework, serve as chauffeur for the various sports practices and lessons, and get dinner on the table—while he relaxes or goes fishing. We both go to bed happy. It's been one of the smartest arrangements we've ever negotiated.

If you are the morning person and he's the night owl, work your on-call hours that way. If you've ever wondered why God planned it so that opposites attract, you can see one of the reasons coming into play during these preschool-parenting years. This way, one of you can always manage to "mind the store" while the other one kicks back. Keep the teamwork operating by working toward your strengths.

If you're a single parent, or if both you and your spouse are working full-time, these breaks are a little harder to come by. But there's still hope! If you're both working, perhaps you can alternate the evenings (or parts of the evening) you have "kid duty" so one spouse can take a nap. Or consider asking a friend or neighbor to baby-sit for a few hours so you can get some rest.

THE GOLDEN RULES OF SLEEP

According to Dr. Maas, there are four golden rules of sleep we need to know in order to remain fully alert all day:[2]

1. **Get an adequate amount of sleep every night.** Optimistically aim at eight or nine hours, which will allow you to function at peak performance.
2. **Establish a regular sleep routine.** Go to bed every night at the same time. Try to wake every morning, without an alarm clock, at the same time. And don't alter the regimen—not even on the weekends. (Even if you have to turn off the video fifteen minutes before that exciting conclusion!)
3. **Get continuous sleep.** Getting six consecutive

hours of continuous sleep is actually preferable to eight hours of interrupted sleep. This is where it gets dicey for moms and dads—and where the teamwork becomes so important. It's no wonder that parents feel the effects of exhaustion; those interruptions wreak havoc with their minds. For some suggestions on how to help your preschooler settle in for the night—so *you* can get a good night's rest—see chapter 15.

4. **Make up for lost sleep.** This one is most important to parents of young children. Dr. Maas reports: "[Sleep loss] is cumulative. If you lose several hours of sleep on a given night, you will become more and more sleepy in the ensuing days, even though you are once again getting your 'normal' sleep. . . . The important rule is to return to your regular sleep schedule as soon as possible."[3] Don't get into "sleep debt," assuming you can catch up on the weekend. Try to recoup those lost hours during the next day, preferably by taking naps and advancing your bedtime.

These golden rules of sleep lay down the law for you exhausted moms and dads: Until your children are on a regular sleeping-through-the-night schedule, you'll have to sacrifice something to get in a short, daily nap—probably while your little one naps.

. . .

POWER CATNAPS

When parenting small children, you won't often have the luxury of a long nap time. However, I've found that even ten or fifteen minutes of deep relaxation, drifting almost completely to sleep and then waking up with or without an alarm, can be extremely rejuvenating. (Sometimes a hot bath can have almost the same effect.) Even some major corporations are beginning to discover that allowing their employees to "power nap" increases productivity over the long haul.

Thomas Edison used to take eight "catnaps" each day, falling asleep in a chair with ball bearings in each palm, waking when they fell and hit the pie pans he'd placed on the floor beside him. He found this system greatly increased his creativity. And now scientists have proven that our most creative times of day are just before drifting to sleep and when we wake up.

WHISPER A PRAYER

Before any rest time, I like to take a minute to focus on God, remembering who I really am (his daughter) and who he really is (the all-powerful Creator). You could try out my standard tired-mom prayer:

"God, my exhausted mom's brain feels like Genesis 1:1 before you created the world—formless, dark, and void. Hover over me as I sleep, Father, the way

. . .

you hovered over the deep darkness—and create order out of the chaos that is my mind in the same way you created order and beauty out of nothingness."

God, who never sleeps, does silent work on my body and spirit as I let go and trust him.

SOMETHING TO THINK ABOUT

Whether or not you have time actually to go to sleep, it's great to quiet and focus your mind—especially if your day has been especially difficult with interruptions. You might focus your mind on a passage of Scripture from your daily or weekly reading of the Bible or something you heard on the radio or in church.

There's power and renewal in the living Word of God. Try Psalm 127:2-3, which talks about the uselessness of staying up late and getting up early (and this was written *long* before Dr. Maas came up with his sleep rules) and points out that God "grants sleep to those he loves" (NIV). It also indicates that children are a gift from God.

No doubt God knew that well-rested, trusting men and women would most enjoy the reward of children. So take your two gifts—your children and sleep—from God, and lay down to rest.

3

LIFE SUPPORT: 911 FOR PARENTS

If you've bought into the whole SuperParent idea that you can do it all, think again! You need help. To bring the best to your kids during your on-duty hours, you definitely need to schedule in some off-duty hours. And to have time to delight in your kids and make the most of those teachable moments, you'll have to push other activities (like perfect housekeeping) off the agenda in order to create more face-to-face and side-by-side time with your preschooler.

IF YOU'RE THE PRIMARY CAREGIVER
Mom's Day Out
Every stay-at-home parent needs a solid chunk of time off for good behavior every week. Mom's Day Out

programs can supply some time off. If your church or park district doesn't offer such a program, call around until you find one that does! Churches typically offer a morning or afternoon off to parents for free or for a minimal, reasonable fee. And while Mom (or Dad) is taking an extended, guilt-free nap; lunching with a friend; catching up on errands; or getting a haircut, the preschooler is happy as can be. Children enjoy that regularly scheduled playtime with other children.

In-home help

Another way to achieve this is to pay a teenager one afternoon a week to come occupy your little activity machine. If you can swing it financially, hire two teens at the same time—one to do some light house-keeping and one to watch your preschooler. Teenager availability is plenteous in the summer months, but responsible homeschooled teens in your area may be available all year round. For recommendations, talk to other parents, church youth workers, or trusted lo-cal teachers. No matter what their age, baby-sitters should have some basic first-aid knowledge, should enjoy children, and should always have a phone num-ber where one of the parents can be reached.

It may seem hard on your budget to pay for this kind of help, but keep in mind that whatever it costs is probably less than therapy at $100 an hour once you've gone completely around the bend! Most couples find a need to budget for couple time every week or every month; it's important that you recognize the need for your own personal downtime as well.

Another way to solve that tight budget problem is parent swapping. In the days when my preschoolers were keeping me running, I found this worked out wonderfully. My kids loved the regular play dates with my friend's kids—one morning at her house under her care, and one morning at mine.

MOPS

MOPS stands for Mothers of Preschoolers, and many churches host weekly or bimonthly meetings where moms can find support, information, and fellowship with other mothers of small children. Many MOPS programs also offer some time off for moms after their regular meeting is finished. Moms can leave their children in the care of the MOPS workers and can get a few hours of rest and relaxation. Check out the MOPS Web site at www.mops.com if you're feeling desperate for the camaraderie of other mothers in your situation.

BALANCING ACT

If you're parenting a preschooler while trying to hold down a full-time or part-time job, you need these breaks from your kids too—but you may feel guilty about spending too much time away. Life as a working parent can feel like walking a tightrope. Maybe you love your job and can't imagine your life without it—yet sometimes your heart aches when you leave your child with the baby-sitter. Or maybe you wish you could stay home but you work because your family needs that extra income. Whatever the situation, you're fighting to balance the many aspects of your life. Here are a few things to consider.

Realize you're not Superwoman or Superman
As authors Karen Scalf Linamen and Linda Holland say in their book *Working Women, Workable Lives,* "Nobody can have it all—but everybody gets to choose."[4] Decide what is most important to you and your spouse, and be willing to make sacrifices to attain it. If enrolling your kids in music class is crucial to you, agree that you'll get take-out the day of the class so you won't have to worry about dinner. For every new responsibility you take on, be willing to let one old responsibility go. Remember, you're only human!

Consider your options
If the stress of your current schedule is too much, look at alternatives. Are flexible hours, reduced hours, or working from home options for you? Is there a hobby

or skill you can turn into a source of income? (A love for cooking could turn into a catering business; administrative skills could be used for at-home medical transcription.) Talk to other parents of small children about how they balance work and parenting. You may get some creative ideas—and make new friends at the same time.

Choose child care wisely

Nothing can add to your guilt more than dropping your preschooler off someplace he doesn't want to be—or with a person you don't feel comfortable with. In her excellent book *All-Day Care,* Susan M. Zitzman describes four things that make up a good child-care situation, whether it's a large center, an individual provider, a relative, or a nanny:

> Use all the help available to you during these demanding days of parenting a preschooler.

1. A caring caregiver—someone who loves your child.
2. An informed caregiver—someone who is trained (formally or informally) in child development.
3. A smaller group of children and a low adult/child ratio.
4. A balanced program of activities—both structured time and "open" time.[5]

．　．　．

If you're not happy with your current child-care situation, look around. Interview new providers. Ask other parents for recommendations. The time you invest in finding the right situation for your child is worth the peace of mind.

Don't hesitate to use all the help that's available to you during these demanding days of parenting a preschooler. Your ongoing freshness and sanity is essential to making the days happy and productive—for both you and your little one.

4

LIFE SUPPORT: STAYING HEALTHY

When your main focus is on your child, it's easy to forget that you and your spouse need some physical care. Though it won't always be easy to manage good nutrition and exercise, it'll be worth the effort. Your preschooler needs a parent who keeps up with her, after all!

MOVE IT!

Obviously, chasing a preschooler all day may be more aerobic than any formal gym class. You can accelerate that workout by initiating races and fast tag in your yard or the park.

If you love to walk, your child will probably enjoy being strolled in a sturdy stroller (or baby jogger) along with you in good weather, or up and down the corridors of a mall when the weather is bad. If you have older preschoolers, they can walk (or skip or hop) with you. For a spiritual twist on this daily walk, check out the book *Prayerwalk: Becoming a Woman of Prayer, Strength, and Discipline* (WaterBrook) by Janet Holm McHenry. This motivating book encourages parents to expand their prayer life for their families.

You might make exercise a regular outing for you and your preschooler by enrolling in parent-and-child dance or gymnastics classes. Contact your local park district or YMCA for options available in your area.

If it's hard to get out of the house, you and your busy-bodied preschooler could try working out together with a kid-friendly video. This makes your exercise a good play and bonding time simultaneously. Brentwood Music's *Sing, Stretch, and Play* is more geared for your preschooler than for you, but it may get you both going!

If you are an early riser and can get up while your preschooler and your spouse are still snoozing, hit the pavement in your Nikes before the day gets going.

GOOD NUTRITION

Every parent should look after her total nutritional intake, including vitamin supplements. Most fatigued women, especially, need to research combinations of

. . .

amino acids and vitamins that will boost the immune system and help produce energy. But let me warn you: Avoid taking any "natural energy pill" with ephedra or ma huang, no matter how tempted you are to take something promising "instant energy" in order to keep up with your preschooler. Not only can it make your heart race, it's been found to push people with sensitive chemistry into frightening and even fatal manic episodes.

A favorite resource of mine is the *Encyclopedia of Natural Medicine* (Prima Publishing). Of course, you should check with your doctor or a certified nutritionist before taking any herb, vitamin, or medication.

> **Pay attention to the nutrients you're getting through your diet, making sure to incorporate a balance of protein, fruits, and veggies.**

Pay attention to the nutrients you're getting through your diet, making sure to incorporate a balance of protein, fruits, and veggies. Whenever possible, choose whole grains or complete starches (brown rice, oatmeal, potatoes, healthy cereals, whole wheat pita bread) instead of breads made with yeast. I don't worry about using a little real butter or olive oil. Studies show that a little fat in your diet keeps you satisfied much longer! And it sure makes food taste better. For a good, commonsense guide on nutrition for the whole family, check out *The Family Nutrition Book: Everything You Need to Know about*

25

Feeding Your Children from Birth through Adolescence by William and Martha Sears (Little Brown).

Desserts are nice treats once in a while, but you know the score: The less sugar and the more healthy ingredients, the better you'll feel. Of course there are those days when nothing but chocolate will do. Just make sure you get really good quality chocolate (rather than quantity) and savor it slowly! If you are a chocolate connoisseur, ask for gift certificates from www.godiva.com for your birthday. Your gourmet chocolate arrives on ice, in a Styrofoam container! It's very impressive.

WETTING YOUR WHISTLE

With bottled water everywhere now, it's easy to get hooked on the clean, refreshing taste of good ol' H_2O. Most doctors recommend drinking at least eight glasses a day. Try putting a few half-filled plastic bottles in the freezer. The water freezes into ice. Then you can fill to the brim with water and keep a drink cold for hours.

I've finally given up all soft drinks—regular and diet. It took me a while to discover that the Nutra-Sweet in diet sodas gave me awful headaches and the sugar content of regular soft drinks went straight to my hips. It's amazing how little I miss them, now that they're out of the picture.

• • •

Caffeine always seems to be in the news, with various studies and reviews in scientific literature coming in with various and opposite results. But the general wisdom from most experts is that we can tolerate one or two cups of coffee a day well. For most people, that's enough to clear the morning cobwebs and lift the mood. I tend to be lethargic by nature, so caffeine doesn't seem to over-rev my system. But many people find that caffeine makes their heart race, gives them the jitters, adds to PMS symptoms, affects their nursing infants, and ultimately brings them up only to send them crashing down an hour later. So you be the judge. Watch your own reaction to caffeine intake, and be cautious. Avoid having more than two cups of coffee daily.

Juice, for both you and your preschooler, is best mixed half-and-half with water. I love orange juice in the morning, but I know it's loaded with sugar—although it's in the form of natural fructose. To cut back on my sugar intake, I mix orange juice, half-and-half, with sparkling mineral water. It's delicious, bubbly, and the children love it too. This works equally well with grape, apple, and pineapple juices.

WOMEN, ANTIBIOTICS, AND YEAST
The female body is a delicate balance, easily upset by nutritional, hormonal, and chemical changes.

One danger area is the long-term use of antibiotics, for whatever reason. Extended use of antibiotics can deplete a woman's body of good bacteria and can lead to a persistent and dangerous yeast overgrowth (*Candida*, which can lead to out-of-control PMS, bloating, fatigue, unexplained weight gain, and frequent infections). For years I suffered from this undiagnosed, though common, yeast overgrowth affecting my digestive system. Now that it's been treated, my weight is down and my energy up—which makes me automatically a more pleasant mother and wife.

TAKE TWO AND CALL ME IN THE MORNING

Both moms and dads should make a point of getting routine checkups plus a complete physical every two or three years. If you can, find a family doctor you feel comfortable with who can treat your whole family. It will simplify things to have all your medical records in one spot!

As a parent, it's easy to be concerned about your child's every sniffle but ignore your own symptoms. Take time to go to the doctor regularly, and make sure you take your own illnesses seriously. The healthier you are, the more energy you'll have for your family.

Take the time to take care of yourself—as a gift to your preschooler, your spouse, yourself, and the rest of your family and friends.

5

LIFE SUPPORT: LIVING SIMPLY

Jackie Gleason used to give advice for rolling with life's punches: "Just play the melody!" There is a season, after all, for complicated harmonies and attention to musical detail. And there's a season for managing the fundamentals.

When it comes to mixing parenthood and homemaking, "just play the melody" is a great rule of thumb. Yes, your house used to be cleaner (okay, *a lot* cleaner) before stuffed animals, Duplo blocks, and stacking rings came to live at your address. Most mothers of preschoolers spend twice as much time just picking up and putting away as they spent cleaning the house before their child reached this energetic play stage.

Some people find housework to be restful or stress-relieving. How wonderful for them! But for those of us who find the necessary housekeeping overwhelming during these years with a preschooler, we need to console ourselves that there will be other years for gourmet dinners à la Martha Stewart.

Obviously, with a preschooler or two in the house, your standards will have to be adjusted. If this relaxed standard drives you or your spouse slightly crazy, take time to talk about which little messy spots make up your pet peeves and give those your first attention. But you'll find, for sanity's sake, that you may not be able to dust and change the bedsheets every week or that you can stretch the time between vacuuming with a little crumb denial!

"I HATE HOUSECLEANING" HINTS

Cleaning house is not my favorite pastime. (I'd rather curl up with a good book.) But over the years I've developed a few survival strategies for keeping the stress of clutter and grime at bay. See if any of these will work at your messy house:

The clean sweep. The "clean sweep" involves literally doing a quick grab-and-run through the house to get all the clutter up and out of sight before dinnertime. This can become a part of your daily routine that allows you a more relaxed dinner hour. I have been known to literally sweep toys into a closet with a huge broom and shut the door. (You may have to lean on it really hard.) Keeping a large basket handy for stray smaller toys is a great help during the clean-sweep time of day.

The play disguise. While you're down on the floor to play with your preschooler, take the opportunity between building blocks or assembling puzzles to sort out and put away other toys within reach. Your child still has most of your attention, and you get a little something done at the same time. Using this same work-and-play technique, lots of moms clean their bathrooms while their preschoolers are splashing in the tub.

Whistle while you work. On my Cheerful Mother Days, I'd enlist the kids' help by singing the tidying-up song "A Spoonful of Sugar," from *Mary Poppins,* in my best English-nanny soprano. I also managed a pretty good dwarf imitation with a rousing rendition of "Hi-ho, Hi-ho, to clean our room we go!" The kids loved it until they hit about age seven, when my singing suddenly embarrassed them. So, at that point I began using my singing as a threat: "If you don't clean your room, I'm gonna start with the SHOWTUNES!" This was guaranteed to send them scrambling for a broom and dustpan.

Contain it. Invest in a set of different-sized plastic bins for toy storage—and teach your kids how to use them! Clear bins will provide a place for clutter but still allow your child to see what's inside—thus alleviating his need to dump all the contents on the floor. Plastic jars with lids can be good containers for small items like marbles.

One a day. Organize one drawer or shelf per day. Amazingly, accomplishing just a five-minute task helps you regain a feeling that you're still in control—of something, anyway!

Time out. Decide how much time you can spend on household chores on a given day—fifteen minutes? an hour?—and set a timer. You'll work more efficiently when you know there's a definite ending point ahead.

Maid to order. If your budget will allow it, hire a housekeeper to come in one to four times a month. If housecleaning isn't your thing but money is too scarce for hired help, see if you can trade a day of housecleaning for baby-sitting, cooking, running errands, etc. with a friend who loves to clean and would be happy to clean your house.

Do it together. The main goal is to have lots of interactive time with your child; a secondary goal is to have a clean, livable home. Let those two goals intermingle. When you're dusting, take a second soft rag for your preschooler and ask her to wipe the legs of the furniture—just her height! When you're sweeping, let him hold the dustpan. When you're paying the bills, let her play "bill-paying" with your throwaway papers, then finish up by letting her help you put on return-address labels and stamps.

Teamwork. Sit down with your spouse and decide who will be responsible for which chores. Then create a job board or mark job "due dates" on a large calendar in the kitchen.

GETTING DINNER ON THE TABLE—AGAIN

Inspirational speaker and humorist Liz Curtis Higgs offers this classic recipe for casseroles: Take everything on the left half of your refrigerator. Combine it with everything on the right half. Sprinkle with potato chips and bake at 350 degrees.

Every parent knows that 6:00 P.M. panic when you realize you've been so busy with your work and your child that you haven't given supper a moment's thought. It's hard to make dinner a priority in these busy days. Here are a few tips for getting yet another dinner on the table.

> Accomplishing just a five-minute task helps you regain a feeling that you're still in control.

Personal best. Start a handy file of recipes that are easy but make you look good! Where to find the recipes? Start by asking other moms for their top two standby supper menus or recipes. Pick up church cookbooks, which are a treasure trove of tried-and-true recipes. Or look for one of the many "fast" cookbooks in bookstores today that highlight entrées that can be ready in twenty minutes or less.

As you experiment, highlight favorite recipes. Write notes in the margins about how long this *really* took or how your family responded so you'll remember the next time.

Head start. One way to get a head start on dinner plans is to season and cook up some hamburger or chicken breasts (cut into one-inch pieces) early in the day, while you're busy with other, everyday kitchen tasks like loading the dishwasher or unloading groceries. Later, you can use the precooked meat in a speedy finish by stuffing pitas or potatoes, or putting it in spaghetti or chili, sloppy joes or Hamburger Helper. A summer favorite at our house is to sprinkle the meat on top of salads—especially lettuce and tomato salad tossed with beans.

Quick dip. My kids love sautéed chicken breast pieces dipped in barbecue sauce or honey. I fix these from frozen chicken breasts in no time at all, by slightly thawing in the microwave, chopping, and browning in a skillet with a bit of olive oil.

Breakfast for dinner. Bacon, eggs, and grits—or French toast and leftover lean ham slices—has saved many a hectic night when I don't feel like cooking or forget to plan a real meal.

That's amore! My husband and kids love frozen pizzas (baked, of course) when I dress them up with extra toppings and cheese and serve with a simple salad or apple slices.

South of the border. Flour tortillas filled with cheese, a little hot sauce, and just about anything else (beans, chicken, scrambled eggs), then folded over and microwaved or sautéed in a little butter, are yummy and quick. My family calls these "Gobblers."

Sweet treats. For quick desserts, there's always ice cream with fun toppings. We also like instant banana pudding, fresh fruit topped with real whipped cream, freeze 'n bake cobblers, or even a bowl of cereal or oatmeal with raisins. These desserts offer a bit more nutrition than cakes, cookies, and candies, anyway!

The Freeman special. For a fast, delicious, not-too-bad-for-you dessert or breakfast treat, cut up an apple and place it in a microwavable bowl. Top it with

1 large marshmallow, 1 teaspoon of brown sugar, 2 teaspoons of butter, and 3 tablespoons of uncooked quick oatmeal. Cover with plastic wrap, then microwave for two or three minutes until the apples are tender. Top with milk or cream.

Planning WAY Ahead

Do you hate to stop at the grocery store every other day because you forgot one ingredient for tonight's dinner? Do you wish you could go weeks without having to cook—but still serve your family homemade meals? If so, check out *Once-a-Month Cooking* by Mimi Wilson and Mary Beth Lagerborg (Broadman and Holman). These two moms give you tips and recipes to help you shop, prepare, and cook meals for one month—all in one weekend! Completed meals are stored in the freezer and can be heated up each night.

TAKE A DAY OFF

It takes a lot of work—by both the parents in the family—to keep a family and its household in good functioning order. So I know the possibility of giving you both a complete day of rest once a week (typically Sunday, for those who choose to worship) may seem ludicrous at first mention. Still, I hope you'll consider it.

God, who created the earth, spent his week of creation working for six days and resting and reflecting on one. It wasn't because he was tired—after all, he's all-powerful. He did it to create a "Sabbath" pattern of work and rest that's healthy for everyone. So try keeping the cooking and cleanup simple and minimal on Sunday—and don't even touch the washer and dryer! You'll be amazed at how much you'll grow to appreciate your time off—and at how much attention and energy become available for the days that follow.

WHAT MATTERS MOST

The following was cross-stitched on a plaque in my children's room. I memorized and recited it often to myself. Perhaps you might want to set it to memory too.

> *Dishes and dusting can wait till tomorrow,*
> *For children grow up, I've learned to my*
> * sorrow.*
> *So quiet down, cobwebs, and dust, go to*
> * sleep.*
> *I'm rocking my baby, and babies don't keep.*
>
> ANONYMOUS

. . . 6 . . .

HEALTHY HABIT: ESCAPING THROUGH BOOKS AND MUSIC

We've covered some ideas that will give you immediate help to stay sane—ways to get some extra rest, to get a break, to keep yourself physically healthy, and to keep the house running with a minimum of disasters. Now let's look at some healthy habits you can develop that will enrich your life—mentally, spiritually, and emotionally. These are habits that will help you grow as an individual and as a parent—habits that will remind you that there is a life outside of parenting.

When you have a preschooler, your life can sometimes feel as narrow as your own four walls. Because your child needs time at home—and especially if your child still naps—your schedule is necessarily some-what limited.

At the same time, many of your friends are busy with their small children and their jobs. It's not always possible to get out and be with others as much as you'd like or need. In times like those, books and music can give you a sense of escape.

FEED YOUR NEED TO READ

Sometimes all it takes to get a break from your hectic day and the give-and-take of preschooler conversation is to pick up a good book! I've found, during times of special frustration or need, that certain books have spoken to my situation exactly. The result is calming—a fresh perspective.

Whether or not you were a great reader before your child reached his preschool years, there's no time like now to discover good books. You'll find that a book that helps you becomes just like a dear and trusted friend. I've compiled this list of great reads to help you get back on track, enjoying parenthood to the fullest.

Take-care-of-yourself books

It's a parent's joy and privilege to pour out her life and energy for those wonderful children God has brought to her family. Because of that, Mom and Dad sometimes need convincing before they take time to care for themselves. Remember, keeping Mom and Dad healthy and happy isn't selfish; it's survival! Here's a short list of titles to reinforce your clear thinking on this point:

If Mama Ain't Happy Ain't Nobody Happy by Lindsey O'Conner (Harvest House)

What Every Mom Needs by Elisa Morgan and Carol Kuykendall (Zondervan)

Pick up a classic

On the first Easter of my husband's and my life as a married couple, my mom handed over her well-worn copy of Edith Schaeffer's *What Is a Family?* (Baker Book House). If you ever need encouragement as you undertake your role as a parent, find a copy of this book. Edith Schaeffer elevates motherhood to priceless ministry. Even after all these years, her book moves me and poignantly reminds me that what I am doing is irreplaceable and of eternal importance.

> Sometimes all it takes to get a break from your hectic day is to pick up a good book.

If the hours with your preschooler are causing you to forget all words over one syllable in length, consider reading some literary or spiritual classics to challenge yourself mentally. Here are a few ideas:

Mere Christianity by C. S. Lewis
My Utmost for His Highest by Oswald Chambers
The Lord of the Rings by J. R. R. Tolkien
Pride and Prejudice by Jane Austen

Inspiring moms

There have been a lot of incredible Christian mothers in the history of the church. For a fresh look at some of these moms who managed to do a great job with their kids, check out Lindsey O'Conner's book *Moms Who Changed the World* (Harvest House). It's written, in part, as a biographical time-travel—a unique and refreshing approach among books for mothers.

Professional moms

If you are currently staying at home full-time, having left a career in order to serve as your children's caregiver, you may miss the professionalism and organization of your old "real" job. Jill Savage, the founder of Hearts at Home Conferences, has written an excellent book called *Professionalizing Motherhood* (Zondervan).

> Music that lifts you up to praise or worship can lift you right out of the effort of parenting.

If you're trying to juggle motherhood with a part-time or full-time job, you know how important it is to prioritize your activities and find time for everything. Here are some resources that can help:

. . .

Working Women, Workable Lives by Karen Scalf
  Linamen and Linda Holland (Harold Shaw)
All-Day Care by Susan M. Zitzman (Harold Shaw)
*Balancing Act: How Women Can Lose Their Roles
  and Find Their Calling* by Mary Ellen Ashcroft
  (InterVarsity)

If you are a left-brain woman, used to control and order, no doubt the pandemonium of a house with a preschooler can get on your last nerve. Pick up a copy of Debi Stack's book *Martha to the Max!* (Moody Press). Debi has a great sense of humor, and if you are even slightly touched with the tendency to perfectionism, you'll enjoy her book.

Fatherhood
Many dads want to learn about the special ways they can bond with their kids. There are several great resources out there:

Seven Secrets of Effective Fathers by Ken R. Canfield
  (Tyndale)
101 Secrets a Good Dad Knows by Walter Browder
  and Sue Ellin Browder (Rutledge Hill Press)
Be There! by John Trent (WaterBrook)

Free and refreshing
The new ideas and personalities you'll meet in the pages of good books will blow through your mind like

the fresh breeze comes through your windows on a spring day. And all that pleasure and encouragement doesn't have to be expensive. Perhaps you and your spouse are trying to make it on one income. Even if you both are working, whether part- or full-time, you probably have a budget you're trying to keep on track. So make that library work for you. Don't hesitate to ask your librarian to track down a book that's not available in your local library. Most libraries are linked in a large system, and these helpful librarians can get you loaners from far and wide! Also, many churches have lending libraries—and they'll allow you to browse and borrow even if the church isn't the one you typically attend. Also, don't be shy about asking a friend to loan you a book she's reading—when she's finished, of course.

You'll find that you'll build a list of books that feel just like old friends—a comfort and encouragement right when you need it.

THE SOUND OF MUSIC

Music is a heaven-sent gift to perk up your mood, and it can have a big effect on your children, too. The CD in your stereo can set the atmosphere for your home.

Listen to lots of different sounds—classical, contemporary Christian, jazz, silly kids' songs, worship music, country, etc. As you listen, notice which CDs energize you and which ones make you relaxed. Take note of the songs that are uplifting, those that are thought-provoking, and those that move you to tears. As you gather this information, you can start to put together your own music therapy kit! Pick a couple CDs for each mood, and make sure they're in an easy-to-find place so you can get them when you need them.

My picks

Everyone has their special tastes, but if I had a tired mom on my front porch and wanted to send her off with some music to set her toes tapping and get her heart ready to waltz with her little ones again, here are the three CDs I'd tuck into her diaper bag as she left:

■ *Songs from a Parent to a Child* by Art Garfunkel (Sony). This recording secured a Grammy for the Best Musical Album for Kids in 1998. It's a CD that both parents and kids will enjoy waking up to in the morning—upbeat, soothing, and tons of fun. It's a real treat to hear Art's son (a miniature, fuzzy-haired version of his dad) belt out a tune with his daddy and deliver a giggle at the end of "Good Luck Charm"—it will charm any parent and child. Kids may love Barney, but that purple dinosaur voice can drive *you* up the wall. It's nice to find an album that parents and kids can enjoy together. From the lovely "Morning Has Broken" to the toe-tapping "You're a Wonderful One" to the reverent "Lord's Prayer," this CD is one of my all-time favorites, even though I'm fresh out of preschoolers in my house.

- *Hold You, Mommy* by 2Moms. These two Texas gals named Laurie and Sharon, sisters and real moms of preschoolers themselves, have formed a dynamite singing duo. These tunes will nourish a mother's heart.
- *Child of the Father* by Cheri Keaggy (Sparrow). This loving mother writes and sings songs that soothe and lift my heart toward heaven. Her pleasant voice holds a childlike wonder. The song "Little Boy on His Knees" touches the heart of every parent who hears it.

There are vast quantities of praise and worship music currently available from Christian music companies—check out the selection at your local Christian bookstore. These songs can nourish a parent's hungry spirit and bring home the truth of God's nearness. What could be a better encouragement than to get through each day with God on your side, by your side? Music that lifts you up to praise and worship can lift you right out of the effort of parenting.

... 7 ...

HEALTHY HABIT: KEEP YOUR SENSE OF HUMOR

I learned by having kids that lots of joy and laughter is common when a house is filled with small children—and some of it you cultivate on purpose. In the middle of chaos and ups and downs, how important it is to have a sense of humor!

I learned quite a bit about the actual value of humor from a child psychologist named Joseph Michelli—and I learned it under very humorous circumstances. He was getting ready to take off, clown suit in tow, to cheer up some children in a Russian hospital, along with the more famous Patch Adams. But first he was scheduled to appear on a Hollywood talk show on which I was also slated to appear. After the show, I rode back to the hotel with Dr. and Mrs. Michelli and immediately knew these parents were the genuine article. They called their kids on their cell phone, talking and laughing and obviously, sincerely enjoying their parenthood and their children.

I immediately went home and ordered his book, *Humor, Play & Laughter: Stress-Proofing Life with Your Kids* (Love & Logic). How I wish I'd had this book at my bedside when I was a young mother of preschoolers!

Small children and monkeys are evidence enough that God has a sense of humor!

Humor is a priceless coping gift for harried parents. Here's just a sampling of what humor has been scientifically proven to do for us, according to Dr. Michelli's book:

1. Humor minimizes a distorted perception of danger.
2. Humor helps a person manage anger more effectively, thereby reducing conflict.
3. Humor provides breathing room for constructive, loving, and logical decision making.
4. Humor assists in communicating difficult feelings.
5. Humor enhances feelings of well-being.
6. Humor augments creativity.
7. Humor strengthens social relationships.
8. Humor reduces the physical ravages of stress.

. . .

9. Humor creates a home environment of warmth and joy.

YOU NEED TO LAUGH

It's completely true that laughter is good medicine. Since many of my own books are humorous ones, I get plenty of letters from mothers saying, "Becky, your books made me lighten up!"

You could look for my books, but other humorous Christians have been writing terrific, funny, encouraging books as well. Here's a short list:

- *She's Gonna Blow!* by Julie Barnhill (Harvest House)
- *365 Ways to Connect with Your Kids* by Charlene Ann Baumbich (Career Press)
- *Forever, Erma* by Erma Bombeck (Andrews McMeel)
- *The Adventures of Mighty Mom* by Gwendolyn Mitchel Diaz (Honor)
- *Worms in My Tea & Other Mixed Blessings* (Baptist Sunday School Board) and *Peanut Butter Kisses & Mud Pie Hugs* (Harvest House) by Becky Freeman
- *Help! I'm Being Intimidated by the Proverbs 31 Woman* by Nancy Kennedy (Multnomah)
- *Sometimes I Feel Like Running Away from Home* by Elizabeth Cody Newenhuyse (Bethany House)
- *It's a Mom Thing* by Kendra Smiley (David C. Cook)

FINDING HUMOR IN THE SMALL STUFF

Where do you find something to laugh at on those days when Murphy's Law is in full effect? I often say that small children and monkeys are evidence enough that God has a fabulous sense of humor! Keep a notebook of the funny things your kids say (three-year-olds are nonstop sources of the best side-splitting material). Watch funny programs, like Veggie Tales episodes. Listen to CDs of silly songs (our favorites were Shari Lewis and Lamb Chop's albums; *Silly Songs with Larry, Kids' **Really** Silly Song Sing-Along,* and the Toddlers Sing series are other good ones). Read kids' joke books or other goofy stories out loud. (Try *The Everything Kids' Joke Book* from Adams Multimedia.) Devise silly games with your little ones—like Mom or Dad pretending to be an elephant or a silly monster and running after screaming children. Create some fun!

Before losing your cool, ask yourself, "If I were Erma Bombeck, is there any possibility that this situation might sound funny on paper tomorrow?"

Before losing your cool, ask yourself, "If I were Erma Bombeck, is there any possibility that this situation might sound funny on paper tomorrow?"

HEALTHY HABIT: LIFE OF THE SPIRIT

We already talked about the care and feeding of the parent—in terms of physical nutrition. But if ever there was a time your spirit needed nurturing, these challenging preschool years are that time! You need an almost constant intake of good stuff going into your heart and your head. Jesus said, "Whatever is in your heart determines what you say. A good person produces good words from a good heart" (Matthew 12:34-35).

Scripture, uplifting books, and inspirational audio-tapes all help store good treasure in our minds. The music we talked about in chapter 6 also contributes to the overall lift of your mental computer "input."

. . .

There are also ways to limit negative input. Many people have stopped watching the evening news in order to avoid being blasted by all the worst and most evil happenings of the world condensed and delivered to your mind at 6 or 10 P.M. The newspaper is typically a more well-rounded and balanced source of information—and even if you only get to it once or twice a week you will certainly catch up with all major events and big stories.

QUIET TIME?!

Parents need to snatch their devotional time when they can get it—and there are certainly days when ten uninterrupted minutes will seem like a luxury! You may want to choose a book of the Bible—one of the Gospels, or Psalms, or Proverbs—and read a segment each day. Like a spiritual treasure hunter, I search out and choose one verse from my day's short reading to mull over and pray over during the day, writing it on a note card or in a journal and asking God to help me apply it to my life.

If you're a morning person, set aside time before your little one is up. Find a quiet chair, sit with a cup of coffee or tea, put on a worship CD, and maybe even light a candle as you read the Bible and pray. This time of quiet can refresh you and prepare you for a hectic day.

· · ·

Devotional readings can be a helpful support. One great little book—perfect for parents on the run who want to tuck a book in their purse or diaper bag—is *When the Handwriting on the Wall Is in Brown Crayon* by Susan Lenzkes (Pentecostal Publishing). Or step into your local Christian bookstore and check out either the women's section or the devotional section—both will be loaded with resources to bolster your spirit.

If you can make the time, consider joining a regular Bible study at church. The accountability and support that come from meeting with the same people each week can be phenomenal! Many churches provide child care during these Bible studies. If your church doesn't have a group that fits your schedule, consider looking for a program at a nearby church. National groups like Bible Study Fellowship or Precepts are interdenominational, well-respected, and available in many areas of the country.

BOOKS TO BOOST YOUR PRAYER LIFE

- *Lord, Bless My Child* by William and Nancy Carmichael (Tyndale)
- *When Mothers Pray* by Cheri Fuller (Multnomah)
- *Praying the Bible for Your Child* by David and Heather Kopp (WaterBrook Press/Random House)
- *With My Whole Heart* by Karen Burton Mains (Word)
- *The Power of a Praying Parent* by Stormie Omartian (Harvest House)
- *How to Pray for Your Children* by Quin Sherrer (Regal)

WHISPER A PRAYER

There may have been times in the past and there may be times ahead when you can have longer sessions of prayer, but these preschooler days make short (and continual) praying a more viable option. Keep prayer times simple, just remembering that God is with you. He wants to know your feelings and needs, hear your thanks and praise, and speak to you. Remember how Jesus complimented the humble man who prayed a very short prayer—"Lord have mercy on me!"—and rebuked the man who went on and on and on ad nauseam about his supposed "spirituality." It only took a few words for God to know and understand each of those men's hearts.

> Keep prayer times simple, just remembering that God is with you. He wants to know your feelings and needs, hear your thanks and praise, and speak to you.

The Lord's Prayer (Matthew 6:9-13) is short but packed with foundational ideas for your faith—understanding God's sovereignty and holiness, relying on God's provision and help on this earth, and trusting God for the future.

Even God's own words from heaven on the occasion of his son's baptism were only one sentence long: "This is My beloved Son, in whom I am well pleased" (Matthew 3:17, NKJV).

Your life with God is about living with him in love; it does not involve a time chart showing how long you spent sitting still in prayer or reading and studying the Bible.

In these days of pouring out your life in service and love for your child, focus on the amazing Father's heart that God evidences. Remember that in this relationship, you are the child—and always will be. There are several fine Christian books that can help you understand more about what it means to be loved by God. Try one (or all!) of these:

Abba's Child by Brennan Manning (NavPress)
The Velveteen Woman by Brenda Waggoner (Chariot Victor)
The Sacred Romance by Brent Curtis and John Eldredge (Thomas Nelson)
The Practice of the Presence of God by Brother Lawrence (Image Books)

All of these books, some of them classics, can nourish a weary parent's spiritual soul. My current favorite is *Strong Women, Soft Hearts,* a newer title by Paula Rinehart (W Publishing Group). The segments that make up this fine book make nice reading bites to tuck into your mind and heart as you tuck yourself into bed.

HOPELESSLY DEVOTED TO YOU, GOD

This attention to your inner life with God is perhaps the most crucial for contentment and peace during the hectic days of mayhem created by having a pre-schooler in the home. Whatever happens, whatever your feelings, whatever your insecurities or fears, God is with you to help you, give you direction, comfort you, and love you. You may have a partner in parenting in your spouse, but your number one partner is God's Holy Spirit.

. . . 9 . . .

PROBLEM SOLVING: WHAT'S GOING ON IN THAT LITTLE BRAIN?

Are you feeling better? You've gotten several ideas for ways to find more time for yourself and take care of yourself! Now let's move on to the next challenge: your preschooler. Before we jump into common parenting dilemmas, let's take a look at how young children think.

A little empathy goes a long way, so use your imagination to toddle a mile in your three-year-old's Keds. Half the battle of learning to handle small children without losing your mind comes from understanding the world as they see it from their pint-sized perspective.

FUZZY LOGIC

Swiss psychologist Jean Piaget studied how children think at different ages. Preschoolers fall into the category Piaget termed "the preoperational stage of cognitive development." What does that mean? It means children in this stage have not yet developed logical thought. One specific aspect of this is called "inability to conserve," which means the child doesn't understand that even if an object is made to look different, some of its characteristics remain the same.

If, for example, you take seven red checkers and seven black checkers, line them up in a row and ask your child if there are more black or red checkers, she'll probably say they are the same. But if you push the red checkers into a small heap, then repeat the question, most likely your child will say there are more black checkers.

Take two Play-Doh balls, equal in size. Then roll one out into a long, thin cylinder as the child watches. Odds are he'll tell you the thin cylinder has more Play-Doh.

If you show a child two identical tall glasses of water, the child will say each glass has the same amount. If you pour the contents of one glass into a short, wide container, she'll probably tell you there's more water in the tall glass.

What does this mean to you as a parent? It means

that your preschool children do not think the same way you do! Reasoning and empathy are skills that are on the way, with great strides ahead in the fours and fives. As your child's thinking matures, your parenting will be oh-so-much easier. You can actually begin to negotiate with a five-year-old. You can say, "If you pick up your toys now, you can stay up fifteen more minutes," and they can anticipate that, visualize it, and respond appropriately. But a two- or three-year-old simply can't see the logic in any request that requires that they give up what they are enjoying right now.

> Creatively and calmly guide your little prince or princess from one activity to another by becoming adept at the fine art of distraction.

So what's a parent to do? Be aware of how your child thinks, and keep in mind his limitations.

LIVING IN THE MOMENT

Little ones exist solely in the here and now. This is one of the qualities that makes this age-group so charming—a butterfly in flight is beyond fascinating, a "rainbow" on an oil slick is cause for celebration. They teach us how to "live in the moment" to the fullest. However, the downside is that when it's time to say "Bye-bye" to the butterfly or the rainbow, this is tragedy!

To try to reason with a two- or three-year-old is an

exercise in frustration. He not only can't understand your logic, he is egocentric—which means self-focused. This doesn't mean he's selfish but rather that he isn't able to see another person's viewpoint. He still believes in the "magic" of his own desires dictating circumstances. He believes that if he states his wish—to stay, to play, to eat Froot Loops for dinner—then his wish will come true!

Fortunately, that live-in-the-moment quality of small children works in your favor. You can use it to help your child move along to other activities because these little people are quite easily distractible. To save yourself days full of frustration, practice distraction techniques. "Hey, Jakey, look over there! Let's race to that tall flower up there on the road." "Let's go call Grandma and tell her what we just saw!" "Let's go upstairs and throw the tub toys into the tub!" If you convey a note of enthusiasm for the next activity, your little one will catch it and follow you into it.

This also comes in handy as your little one learns the give-and-take of sharing. When two little people are in a death struggle over the same toy, you can produce another old favorite or two to distract them. Or, when your little one has fixated on some food you don't want to feed him at lunchtime, you can produce a brightly colored yogurt package. Distraction still works!

· · ·

DON'T TAKE IT PERSONALLY

When your preschooler shouts "No!" or "I hate you!" go ahead and discipline the outburst, but don't take it personally or assume that the child is emotionally mature enough to understand what he has said. Ignore the remark, and respond calmly but firmly. Don't fall in the trap of knee-jerk reactions, or you'll find yourself arguing on the level of a two-year-old. This is *not* a pleasant experience, and all parents at one time or another have found themselves falling into this trap. Here's another good reason to get the rest and care you need for yourself: It makes it easier to distance your emotions from your preschooler's at a time like this.

Remember, these little ones who are living in the moment are feeling all the keen disappointment of the tragedy of, say, having to go home from a friend's or having to eat chicken. They want so much to enjoy and control their world, and those words "I hate you" really translate to "I hate what you are making me do! I wanted to be king of all I survey!" As Lawrence Kutner, psychologist and award-winning parenting columnist, writes, "The fundamental job of a toddler is to rule the universe."[6]

HANG ON TO YOUR SENSE OF HUMOR

Take it all in stride with a healthy sense of humor. Be the creative adult and calmly guide your little prince or princess from one activity to another by becoming adept at the fine art of distraction. Humor is the ultimate form of distraction. Say something outrageous. Do something silly. At least until the day your child realizes a dime is worth more than a nickel, even though it's smaller. At that point, you will know that her brain is ready to begin reasoning with you.

PROBLEM SOLVING: POTTY TRAINING

When I was mothering my first preschool child, a book called *Toilet Training in Less than a Day* was making the rounds of hopeful parents. I was surprised to find that the book is still in print now, although reviews from parents are mixed, if not polarized. Though there were some great techniques in the book, such as celebrating your child's accomplishments when he keeps his pants dry, I never personally met even one parent who could claim that the job was actually finished in one day.

All good toilet-training books emphasize waiting for readiness, and this is vitally important. To start too soon is an invitation for trouble. In fact, author and parenting expert Brenda Nixon points out that toilet training is one of the parental stresses that most often leads to child abuse![7]

Generally, little girls tend to potty train earlier (sometimes as early as age two or two and a half); boys tend to potty train more easily much closer to age three. Nixon, in her book *Parenting Power in the Early Years*, points out that research published in *Pediatrics* magazine revealed that only 4 percent of children are out of diapers by age two, a whopping 82 percent by age three, and only 2 percent weren't trained by their fourth birthday.[8] Save yourself the unnecessary aggravation and don't even start trying to toilet train a child until he is at least two and a half.

> Gentle prodding and rewarding, when your child is truly ready on his own timetable, is usually just as effective as specialized training techniques.

Gentle prodding and rewarding, when your child is truly ready on his own timetable, is usually just as effective as specialized training techniques.

These days, the availability of disposable Pull-Ups can help parents and preschoolers transition from diapers to underwear. Little ones love the feel of wearing "big-kid pants."

There are training potties for all preferences. There are pint-sized potty chairs for kids who like to have a "throne" just their size. To other kids, the appeal is going in the big potty—especially enjoying the *whish!* of the flush. For these children, be sure to use a nifty plastic insert to keep their little bottoms from falling down into the water!

For parents who are frustrated with yet another potty-accident cleanup, it's easy to let temper or irritability become the guiding principle of your potty training. Don't fall into this trap. Try to keep the atmosphere as light as possible. Some parents help their sons potty train by making a "shooting" game out of potty time. Try floating a Cheerio or a piece of toilet paper in the toilet bowl, and have your son do some target practice!

Children who have big brothers and sisters tend to train most easily. So, if your own modesty permits, invite your small trainer into the bathroom with you. Or

---

BEST POTTY BOOKS TO READ TO YOUR KIDS

- *The Potty Book for Girls* and *The Potty Book for Boys* by Alyssa Satin Capucilli (Barrons)
- *My Big Girl Potty* by Joanna Cole (HarperCollins)
- *My Big Boy Potty* by Joanna Cole (HarperCollins)
- *Once Upon a Potty* by Alona Frankel (HarperCollins). There are his and hers versions of this classic.
- *Caillou-Potty Time* by Joceline Sanschagrin (Chouette)
- *Flush the Potty* by Ken Wilson-Max (Cartwheel). Includes a button your child can press that gives a satisfying flushing sound.
- *I Can Go Potty* by Bonnie Worth (Golden Books). Features Kermit the Frog.

let your child interact with preschoolers who have already achieved potty-training success—either in Sunday school, Mom's Day Out, or in play groups. Peer pressure at work at this early stage encourages your child to use the potty—because she saw her friends doing it.

. . . 11 . . .

PROBLEM SOLVING:
FINICKY EATERS

I was surprised to learn that children actually taste things differently from adults. Their taste buds are more sensitive, so they might be overpowered by the spiciness of a dish their parents might consider bland. Young children in particular do not seem to like bitter tastes, such as those found in dark green vegetables.

But many, many parents wring their hands in near-despair when their preschooler refuses any foods—except, say, peanut-butter-and-jelly or egg-salad sandwiches—for weeks at a time.

The best advice seems to be, "Don't panic!" Dr. Lawrence Kutner says, "As long as your child is generally healthy and isn't losing weight, you have nothing to worry about."[9] Remember that as long as their nutritional needs are met throughout a week, they are going to survive and thrive—even if they seem to eat mostly fruit on Monday, peanut butter on Tuesday, and so on. Even if they are not eating a wide variety of vegetables, they may be getting the fiber and nutrients through fruit.

For good measure, do supplement your child's food with a chewable children's multivitamin.

Most preschoolers accept milk, yogurt, and eggs happily. That's great, because these are packed with nutrition and will help non–meat eaters get their protein needs met.

Don't force your kids to eat when they aren't hungry. However, when they are very hungry, take advantage of this by offering the most nutritious foods first.

> Young children in particular do not seem to like bitter tastes, such as those found in dark green vegetables.

Preschoolers love to do "big people" things with you—like food preparation. You can take advantage of this by allowing your little chef to help you prepare nutritious snacks. Sometimes being involved in the creating—or picking of fresh veggies and fruits—heightens a child's interest in trying new foods.

Check out cookbooks that specialize in fun-looking

foods that kids like. In her book *Parenting Power in the Early Years,* Brenda Nixon recommends the following cookbooks:

- *Feeding Your Child for Lifelong Health: Birth through Age 6* by Susan B. Roberts, Ph.D., and Melvil Heyman, M.D. (Bantam Doubleday Dell)
- *One Bite Won't Kill You: More than 200 Recipes to Tempt Even the Pickiest Kids on Earth* by Ann Hodgeman (Houghton Mifflin)

Four of my favorite kitchen resources are:

- *Feed Me! I'm Yours* by Vicky Lansky (Meadowbrook)
- *The Taming of the C.A.N.D.Y. Monster* by Vicky Lansky (Book Peddlers)
- *Food for Little Fingers* by Victoria Jenest (St. Martins)
- *Incredible Edible Bible Story Fun* by Jane C. Jarrell and Deborah L. Saathoff (Group)

Kids love minifoods. I used to make small pizzas out of bread dough, and let the kids "decorate" their own with cheese and toppings. For older preschoolers, who have learned to chew their food well, miniature hot dogs (cocktail wieners), baby carrots, and mini-sandwiches cut into fun shapes can also be big hits.

Almost anything you are serving can be arranged

on a child's plate in a fun way! Did you ever cut eyes and a smile in a slice of lunchmeat? See the book *Play with Your Food* by Joost Elffers and Saxton Freymann (Stewart, Tabori & Chang) for other ideas.

Most children love fruit smoothies, even if they aren't big fruit eaters. I keep bananas (peeled and wrapped in plastic) in the freezer, then add them to juice or milk and blend it to a milk-shake consistency, often adding a dash of vanilla. My kids called this "Monkey Juice."

Another way to make eating fun for your finicky eater is to put food on a stick. Children enjoy "spearing" cheese chunks with toothpicks, dipping celery, and eating cocktail sausages from the tip of a fork. Most preschoolers are old enough to handle toothpicks and forks, but you'll want to keep these sharp objects away from younger children.

You could also take it outside. Create an impromptu "picnic"—packing finger sandwiches and small foods in a basket to go—even if it's just out to the backyard!

Whatever happens, make mealtime as pleasant as possible. The atmosphere around the table affects your child's hunger and digestion. Can you ever remember a delicious dinner starting to taste like cardboard once a family tiff was underway? Our children are affected by the mood we set at the table too.

. . . 12 . . .

PROBLEM SOLVING: THE DILEMMA
OF THE BITER

I was outraged. When I picked up my child from the nursery, the workers had the sad duty of telling me my sweet little boy had been bitten! Sure enough, the evidence—tiny rows of reddened teeth marks—semi-circled my child's plump toddler arm.

Two years later, I was horrified again. But this time it was one of *my* children who had bitten a playmate when my back was turned for a few brief moments!

Having been both the parent of a child who was bitten and the parent of a child who bit, I can say with all sincerity that it's the parent of the aggressive child who hurts the most. What has she done wrong? How could she have prevented this? How could this little one, who used to be such a precious little bundle in her arms, injure another child in such a primitive way?

First, all parents need to know that many young children go through a biting stage. It's extremely common and doesn't by itself predict later emotional or social problems.

WHY KIDS BITE

In her book *Parenting Power in the Early Years*, Brenda Nixon writes, "Sometimes a toddler bites not to be aggressive or hostile, but to ease the pain of teething. Or he bites for sensory exploration—an educator's term for putting stuff in his mouth to learn about it. The mouth is a powerful information organ, and I've seen kids bite chairs, plants, even the dog. . . . The simple remedy is to give your tot soothing, slobber-resistant chew toys. Teething rings, a wet washcloth, or a Popsicle are safe ways of relieving aching gums as well as satisfying that urge to 'see what it's like.'"[10]

Also, child experts remind us that children are limited in expression at this age. When they get overexcited, angry, jealous, or even especially happy, they sometimes get the urge to bite something—or someone—as a form of communication. Of course, we have to help them stop the behavior; it cannot continue. But it helps to understand that they are acting out of frustration or curiosity, not overt evil or desire to hurt. Also, biting is rarely pre-meditated. Children often simply act without thinking of consequences.

A new trend in teaching babies to use basic sign language may prove to be especially helpful with small children who need ways to communicate their needs before their language skills catch up. For more information, look for *Sign with Your Baby* by W. Joseph Garcia or on the Web at www.babysigns.com or www.littlesigners.com.

> In time, your child's ability to express herself in words will take the place of biting.

What's a parent to do?

Obviously, by the preschool years of three, four, and five, you'll want your child to have mastered the skills to communicate frustration without resorting to injuring others.

So when a biting incident occurs, respond swiftly and immediately. Firmly but gently hold the child's face around their jawline, and sternly tell the child, "No! We can bite apples or bagels, but we never ever bite people! See, biting hurt our friend!"

If possible, involve the offender in helping to comfort the child that has been injured, washing any wound with soap and water, applying antibiotic and non-stick Telfa pads. When the injured child is comfortable, turn your attention to the biter. Acknowledge her feelings: "I know you are angry, but . . . " and show her another way to release them. Maybe she can squeeze a squishy stuffed animal, or you can help her find a toy or game to take her mind off the situation.

In time, your child's ability to express herself in words will take the place of biting. Encourage her to "use your words!" (Before she becomes proficient in speaking is when the ability to sign basic needs could be a real help.)

Meanwhile, you might enjoy reading the humorous children's story *No Biting, Horrible Crocodile!* by Jonathan Shipton (Golden Books). I wish I'd had this resource when I was struggling to defang my own little biter. Here's what a preschool teacher writes about it: "Our day-care center had a problem with the young children biting. The teachers read this book to the kids every day and the problem disappeared. The kids really seemed to love the story line as well as understand the concept."

It's important for you to hang on to your own temper and keep the biting in perspective. Though repulsive to parents, biting is a normal behavior for toddlers and some young preschoolers. Usually the injury is minimal (albeit painful) and doesn't break the skin. The victim normally just needs a hug, the biter a swift and firm "No!" Spanking the child has not been shown to be particularly effective. (Take it from this mother who tried it without success!) While it may seem like your child is too old for such things, some little ones do stop biting behavior when they are allowed to use a pacifier or teething toy.

13

PROBLEM SOLVING:
ENCOURAGING CREATIVITY

In my book *Peanut Butter Kisses and Mud Pie Hugs*, I devote a chapter to creativity in families. In it, I describe the incredible freedom to explore and create that Steven Spielberg's mother allowed—even applauded—in their family. Who knows if your three-foot finger painter will become the next Monet? Your daughter playing dress-up and pretending may become a great Shakespearean actress. Even if they never become famous, a lifetime of joy comes from the seed of creativity birthed and encouraged in their younger years.

Much of a child's creativity—if not all of it—comes in the form of creative play. Keep this in mind as you

. . .

choose playthings for your preschooler. The more imagination a toy or activity requires, the better. As a child I spent many happy hours envisioning and creating homemade dollhouses. I loved it! Then I was given a beautiful, "professional" dollhouse. Soon afterward, I quit playing dollhouse. Why? Though it was unintentionally done, the joy of being involved in the creative process was taken away from me. It's the process, not the product, of play that children love most.

Remember, too, that the best toys have always been free (or inexpensive). Here's a short list of creative pastimes that primarily use things you have around the house or cheap garage-sale items.

- **Play-Doh fun.** Plastic knives and forks, cookie cutters, plastic place mats and floor mats—and Play-Doh (which you *can* make yourself, if you're ambitious!).
- **Sandbox delights.** Pails, sifters, shovels—and sand, of course.
- **Dress-up box.** Old clothes, hats, shoes, wigs, sunglasses, etc.—and a mirror in which to admire your ensembles.
- **Water!** In the bathtub, yard, pool, or sprinkler; with bubbles, water balloons, squirt guns, old spray bottles, etc.

- **Craft box.** Old greeting cards, kid scissors, bits of colorful paper, stickers, markers, glue, glitter, paint, an old oversized T-shirt (smock), and a big table—or floor—where messes are acceptable.
- **Building toys.** Puzzles, Duplos, and big plastic or wooden blocks. If you've got the time, collect interesting lumber scraps left at a construction site. Sand 'em down. My own boys loved these.
- **Fort/House/Store.** Materials to create tents (old blankets or sleeping bags); a pretend store (empty boxes taped up, play money, and a cash register); blanket over the kitchen table; couch cushions; sticks; scrap lumber and plywood in the yard; big empty boxes from appliance stores.
- **Puppets.** An instant puppet theater can be made by draping a sheet over a low dresser. You can make hand puppets out of socks and sacks, or stick puppets of paper figures attached to Popsicle sticks (or wooden spoons). Or hang a sheet and cut shapes out of black paper; backlight the sheet to create a shadow-puppet theater.

If you do invest in new toys, you might consider shopping at teacher-supply stores, where the toys tend to be sturdy, educational, and have long-lasting appeal.

. . .

BOOKS

Even though most preschoolers are not ready to read, they will love to peruse picture books and have you read to them. Reading to your child can be a wonderful first step in helping him learn to read and write himself. Point out letters and numbers as you read, or show her which words match the pictures on the page. For ideas of activities you can do to interest your child in reading, try *Creating Readers* by Pam Schiller (Gryphon House).

Get over to your local library and help your kids get comfortable with a routine of borrowing books—and taking good care of them. Many libraries provide suggested reading lists, including award-winning books for kids of all ages. In addition, librarians can help you find books on a particular subject your child is interested in.

It's also great to have these treasures in the house—ones your kids can own and keep in their rooms. Inexpensive books are available at thrift stores, church bazaars, and garage sales. Make your budget, and then make a book-buying day of it. Stop at cheap places, buy your books, then have burgers or ice cream out. Back at home, help your kids set up their own milk crates of book treasures in their rooms, where they can easily flip through their purchases. By nap time, you'll be snuggling up to read through a couple of your new book friends. If you are excited about reading, your child will be too.

When you're reading to your child, take time to look at the illustrations and talk about which ones you like, noticing clever details and beautiful colors. Some of the best, most affordable art is right there in your children's quality books! This is a great chance to initiate them in noticing artistic expression. (Check out past winners of the Caldecott Award for illustrations in a picture book—see the list at www.bookweb.org/news/awards/1295.html.)

Don't limit yourself to fiction stories. Preschoolers are avidly curious. Look for books about plants, flowers, apples, and bees. Seek out books about dinosaurs, fire trucks, trains, and planes. Look for alphabet books, anticipating the skills that are introduced in actual preschool. These books are educational, of course, and they're great fun. Some of these books about real life have fabulous photo illustrations—very colorful and dynamic.

Pick up a Bible storybook with age-appropriate illustrations. Your child will love these true stories, adapted from Scripture, for little listeners.

THE ARTS

Think it's too early to get your child involved in music or art? Think again! Even very young children can benefit from learning about music. In fact, the national Kindermusik program includes a course for infants! Several studies have shown that exposure to classical music improves academic performance. Another study indicates that preschoolers' "spatial-temporal reasoning" is improved by six months of piano lessons.[11] Consider enrolling your child in a Kindermusik class or a similar program that will let him or her explore sounds, try out instruments, move to music, and learn new songs. Your child will have a creative outlet, and you'll enjoy this bonding time as well.

If your child is interested in art, find some books that show an artist painting or drawing. Consider taking your preschooler to a child-friendly art museum. And encourage your child to paint, draw, sculpt with clay, or try other artistic pursuits.

Playing "make-believe" with your preschooler can be a good way to encourage imagination and drama. Try acting out the story of a book you've read together, or consider taking your child to a children's theater performance or a storytelling session at the library.

AVOID OVERLOAD

I recently read a story about a little boy who collected small cars. His aunt, wanting to surprise him, found a way to get him *all* the toys in the collection at once.

To her surprise, she found him sitting on his bed, bewildered, not even touching the cars.

"What's the matter?" she asked.

Sadly he replied, "It's just too much to love."

Children are easily overwhelmed with too many toys. Try putting half of their toys up on a shelf, in a closet, or up in the attic, where they are out of sight. Every three or four months, rotate them—it's like taking old friends and making them new again.

> **If you're going to encourage creative play, you'll have to allow for a lot of temporary messiness.**

Also, make toy pick-up—and preschoolers should certainly be helping with cleanup—easy for them to handle. Both you and your child will appreciate big open bins or boxes for toy storage. Open laundry baskets, milk crates, and plastic buckets lined up along the edge of their bedroom walls (not stacked) work better than shelves and drawers—and they make cleanup easy.

GOOD MESSINESS

If you're going to encourage creative play, you'll have to allow for a lot of temporary messiness. Try to make cleanup easy to do, and try to enjoy "creative clutter" during the years you have small children. You'll have more fun and less stress; and they'll have incredible memories of a parent who let them explore the world!

There's a proverb in the Bible that basically says that a stall without oxen stays clean, but it produces no income. A home without children stays clean, but it produces no little human beings to bring joy to the earth!

Preschoolers are busy little bodies. There are lots of books containing activity suggestions. Try *The Preschooler's Busy Book* by Trish Kuffner (Meadowbrook), which offers you 365 days of ideas for keeping your child busy—all for less than $10. Now that's a bargain.

14

PROBLEM SOLVING: DISCIPLINE
WITH GRACE

Two years ago I was asked to emcee, Oprah-style, a very interesting event at Illinois State University sponsored by the large hospital in the area. On the forum that night were two very different child-rearing "experts," presenting two very different ways to raise and discipline children. An obviously conservative couple represented a popular religious-based program. The husband wore a suit, the wife a classic print dress. Their demeanor was kind, gracious, and controlled. Their children seemed well behaved and happy.

The other presenter was a popular radio psychologist, also a Christian. Very laid-back, fun-loving, high-energy. He was dressed in jeans, a casual shirt, and

tennis shoes, and he extolled the virtues of a more relaxed and creative discipline method. His children
seemed well behaved and happy.

My job was to keep the evening light and informative—to keep the event from turning into a debate. I
was pleased and surprised to see how easy that challenge turned out to be. Both presenters were gracious, both admitting that the method they'd chosen
to raise their children worked well, in part, because it
was the method they felt most comfortable using due
to their own personalities.

When it comes to disciplining your children, there
are a dozen excellent "methods," and most likely, you
will end up choosing one that fits your own lifestyle
and personality. As long as there is at least as much
emphasis on loving your children as there is on correcting and training them, you and your children will
do just fine. My mother once told me—wisely, I
think, "Becky, even if you and Scott managed to do
everything perfectly as parents, you'd still raise fully
flawed kids in need of God's grace."

My one heartfelt caution is this: If you find that a
certain method of disciplining your child is leaving
you more and more irritated, frustrated, and angry at
your kid's level of performance—if you feel yourself
turning into Drill Sergeant Dad or Manic Mom—there
is probably an overemphasis on discipline, without

. . .

enough grace, positive reinforcement, humor, and play to balance it all out.

The Old Testament book of Micah puts in a nutshell what pleases God most: "To do justly, to love mercy, and to walk humbly with your God" (Micah 6:8, NKJV).

We are to expect our children to do right; we are to train them to be good and just. But if there is ever this question in your heart when you are correcting a child: "Is this a time for justice or mercy?" and you sincerely don't know the answer, lean toward mercy. In this way, you'll make fewer permanent mistakes. Parents who tend to be more grace-oriented cause less emotional damage than parents who put "behaving right" as the top priority in their home.

> **The key to discipline is balance, balance, balance.**

We are to be people and parents who require justice, for sure, but we also need to be in love with the concept of mercy and grace. Don't forget, we were once children ourselves—children who made our own little red wagonloads-full of mistakes. In fact, we are forever children to God, our heavenly Father. And aren't you glad he deals with us, most often, according to his grace and mercy, and less often according to what we deserve?

Perhaps this is what Micah meant when he said we are to "walk humbly" with our God. The best way to walk humbly is to remember how easily we all fall down.

. . .

HOW TO REALLY LOVE YOUR CHILD

There's a classic parenting book by Dr. Ross Campbell called *How to Really Love Your Child*. If I could put one book in the hands of every parent of a preschooler, this would be the one.

Dr. Campbell points out three vital ways we communicate love to our little people:

1. Eye Contact
2. Physical Contact
3. Focused Attention[12]

In his chapter on loving discipline, Dr. Campbell encourages parents to ask these questions before punishing misbehavior:

1. What does this child need? (Is there a deeper, underlying emotional need?)
2. Is there a physical problem? (Is your child sleepy, sick, hurt, hungry?)
3. Is he genuinely remorseful? (If so, perhaps punishment is inappropriate and forgiveness is called for instead.)[13]

This is a great reminder to parents that we're not doing our preschoolers any favors by messing with their regular nap times, bedtimes, and nutritional meals. We help them behave by giving them the best chance to control themselves. Then, obviously, there are times when we must give them a bit of slack because the answer to these three questions indicates a more important issue than the infraction right at hand.

TO SPANK OR NOT TO SPANK

Parents come down on different sides of this issue—even Christian parents. But if you do choose to spank, it should be very limited indeed by the time your child is four or five. Even professionals who feel that spanking is appropriate agree that it's most productive in the ages before reasoning is possible (one to

---

TIPS FOR HANDLING YOUR ANGER

(condensed from *Toddlers and Preschoolers* by child behavior columnist Lawrence Kutner, Ph.D.)

1. Consider your stress level before tackling a toddler-accompanied event.
2. Schedule generous helpings of downtime—for taking walks, making popcorn, and watching a movie. Overscheduling and time pressure are usually involved in the mix of parents losing their cool.
3. Ask yourself, "Am I expecting too much?" Familiarize yourself with age-appropriate behaviors listed in almost any general child development book.
4. Correct the behavior but don't berate the child.
5. Apologize sincerely when you do lose it. This also models for your children how they can say, "I'm sorry" when they misbehave, be forgiven, and start again.

---

three; most doctors feel that it is never appropriate to spank a child under the age of one). There are many other effective methods of discipline that work well with preschoolers. It's important that you try a number of alternatives in order to determine which method works best for your child.

HANDLING OUTRIGHT TANTRUMS

Tantrums are much more common in the toddler years (eighteen months until about three years), but you may still have preschooler meltdowns now and then.

As always, the best cure is prevention. When kids are tired or hungry, they tend to get cranky more easily (just like you, only they're much more theatrical about it). So use your judgment, and let your child's emotional needs come before your to-do list now and then. For example, if your kid is on his last emotional leg, skip the grocery store and pick up only what you need at a convenience store—even if milk is a little more expensive there. Try to work high-energy events into the day's schedule after her naptime or first thing in the morning. Give your child the optimum chance for success at handling his own ups and downs.

However, when a full-fledged tantrum is in play, and you know her basic needs have been cared for and creative diversion won't work, here are some techniques for handling your child.

Walk away. If you are at home, just leave him alone. Sometimes he just needs a good long hollering sob to get the frustration out of his system. Other times, she'll stop immediately because she knows it's pointless to keep producing great theatrics without an audience. Just get on with your business, moving from room to room, even if the little drama king or queen follows you about, floor-flopping in every room of the house. Eventually, the child will run out of steam.

Don't give in. Many, if not most, tantrums are initiated because a parent has said a firm "no" to something the child wants. Don't ever let your child's fit of bad behavior change your answer. Try saying, "If you would like to talk to me in your nice voice, I can stop and listen to how you feel. But I can't hear screaming or whining."

Limit the time. Set the microwave timer and tell your child she may cry until the bell goes off, but then she'll have to stop. If she doesn't, then she'll have to go to her room with the door closed until she is ready to behave.

Set a time-out. I recommend assigning time-outs of one minute per year of the child's age. A three-year-old can handle three minutes on a chair or bed—away from TV or toys.

Get private. If you're in public when your preschooler melts down, you can't walk away and ignore him. (They arrest parents for stuff like that.) So immediately pick up your child and retreat to somewhere private—like a restroom or your car. Don't even say a word; just quickly remove him from the crowd to where you are his only audience. If people stare, go ahead and smile and say something pleasant in apology, but do what you must to care for the child's needs or enforce discipline, whichever you sense is the greatest need of the moment.

Distract with humor. If your child's meltdown is in reaction to hurting himself with a toy or chair or stairs, or in frustration with a toy that won't operate as it should, try stopping the tears with a bit of humor. Scold the naughty chair or toy in mock disapproval. Most likely, your child will stop crying and start laughing.

A WORD FROM MY HEART

Though we all know kids who are out of control, whose parents seem almost intimidated by their children, I, personally, am more concerned with some of the discipline methods being advocated today in Christian circles. Parents who use these methods are turning out perfectly behaved little children who eerily remind me

· · ·

of robots. These children (parented to the extreme) are super polite, extra cautious, and obviously afraid to make a mistake. While these children may be easy to handle now, many Christian psychologists tell us that these children turn into grown-ups who don't know who they are, what they think, or how they really feel.

Somewhere we must find the happy medium. The key to discipline is balance, balance, balance. A good question to ask yourself is, "Which method of discipline allows me to *like* who I am as a parent? Which method allows both me and my child a sense of self-worth, happiness, dignity, and caring while keeping chaos at bay?" If you grew up in a healthy, loving home and have a wonderful love relationship with God, it could be that you need no "formal" method to follow but that God has given you the simple gift of relaxing, enjoying, and correcting your kids when needed. I call this *parenting by common sense!*

15

PROBLEM SOLVING: BETTER BEDTIMES

BEDTIME BLUES

Bedtime can turn out to be quite the drawn-out or-
deal, especially when dealing with multiple small children. Here are the best hints to get kids to bed so you
can have a little quiet time alone or with your mate.

Keep bedtime the same time every night. In just a few
days of regular bedtimes, your child's internal clock
will be sending "you are tired" messages at just the
right time.

Let the clock's hand be the bearer of bedtime news by
telling your child, "When the big hand gets to the
top, it's time for bed!" This is a good introduction to

telling time, and it makes the clock, not you, "the bad guy."

Rub-a-dub, put the kid in the tub. At least in the summertime, busy preschoolers could use a bath every day. So plan that warm bath right before bedtime. It will relax and warm their little bodies.

Good-night snack. If your preschoolers typically want something to eat before bed, provide milk and low-sugar cereal or oatmeal, which supply your children with natural sleep-inducing carbohydrates.

Good-night parade. Writer Vicki Lansky suggests having a "Good-night Parade"—which is especially fun if you have lots of children and if you can get all the family involved. March through the house, stopping in the kitchen for water, bathroom for tooth brushing and using the potty, and the living room for hugging Mommy or Daddy good night (depending on who's leading the parade). The youngest child, "the caboose," is dropped off first, tucked in bed, and hugged by the others. The oldest child has the privilege of a little "just you 'n me" big-kid chitchat.

Read a bedtime story. Limit the number of books ahead of time, or read one chapter a night. By skipping over some of the more detailed sections and using my most theatrical voices, I read *Little House on the Prairie, Pippi Longstocking, The Boxcar Children,* and several other books to my young preschoolers. My husband, Scott, often read the kids their bedtime story (or, even better, made up a tall tale of some sort). Sometimes he'd read to them on their beds; sometimes they would pile up around him on the big La-Z-Boy rocker. Of course the kids loved their Daddy to tickle and wrestle with them in the evenings. Since that got them more excited than sleepy, I'd always follow Dad's playtime with bath time.

> **Talk with your spouse about how you want to handle kids climbing into bed with you at night.**

Sing to them. I love to sing and, when they were small, my children loved to hear me. I'd put a karaoke-type background tape in the stereo, rock them or lie down with them, and sing my heart out to my favorite soothing love songs or praise songs. My kids used to beg for more! Ah, those were the days.

Good-night music. Play a soothing tape of lullabies or a short children's story that ends with a pretty song of praise. Songs that affirm that God is watching over them and that he loves them are especially good.

NIGHT WAKING

Children very commonly experience night terrors. We found that the best response was to hold and comfort the child, and to pray with them, using phrases like, "Dear Father, we know you protect us and that your angels take care of us even while we sleep . . . " Sometimes we also put on a light or night-light to help ease their fears.

Talk with your spouse about how you want to handle kids climbing into bed with you at night. Different parents have different views and preferences (sometimes based on whether or not they are light sleepers) about whether or not to permit this. Scott and I allowed it frequently, though I have to admit we didn't sleep as well. Still, all of our children have grown up to sleep happily in their own beds, and they are some of the most self-reliant and independent kids you'll ever meet. This decision, like most parenting choices, falls under the category of "do what feels best to you and your spouse." Children are amazingly resilient and adaptable—as long as they are given lots of love and guidance.

16

PROBLEM SOLVING: TEACHING YOUR CHILD ABOUT GOD

Teaching your preschooler about God is one of your most important roles as a parent—and one of the most frightening. Many parents feel overwhelmed by the idea and aren't sure where to start. The good news is that there are a lot of resources out there to help.

DO YOUR HOMEWORK

It can be difficult to know what your child can understand about God and how you can teach him in a way he can understand. Here are a few guidelines to get you started:

Two-year-olds
- Can learn to trust God if they first learn to trust people
- Can understand what God does better than who he is. (For example, they can see what God made but can't understand that he's holy, eternal, etc.)
- Can begin to pray simply

Three-year-olds
- Can learn that God loves them, is with them, and hears them talk
- Can start to understand that the Bible has God's words in it and that we read it and treat it carefully
- Can verbalize prayers more and learn that they can talk to God just as they talk to a parent
- Can know that Jesus was a baby, a boy, and a man; that God is his Father; and that he is in heaven now

Four-year-olds
- Think about God in a personal way and can trust him
- Begin to see the difference between right and wrong; can learn to obey not just because of the consequences but from the satisfaction of doing the right thing

- Can learn that Jesus is God's only Son and is very special
- Readily believe Bible stories about what God does

For more information on how children of different ages think, or for ideas on how to teach these concepts to kids, try these resources:

Parents' Guide to the Spiritual Growth of Children
by Focus on the Family (Tyndale House)
Child Sensitive Teaching by Karyn Henley (Allen Thomas)

Teaching your child about God doesn't have to be hard. Here are some ways you can incorporate it into your daily routines.

PRAY TOGETHER

Make a habit of praying together at regular times throughout the day—perhaps before meals and before bed. Even very young children can learn that talking to God is a special time. By hearing you pray about concerns in your life, your child will grow to understand that God cares about us.

SING TOGETHER

There are lots of great CDs of Christian music for kids. From praise and worship music to silly songs to old

. . .

campfire favorites, kids love to listen and sing along. Singing with your child can also give you an opportunity to talk to her about worship. Explain why we sing to God (to thank him for loving us and always being with us) and how we can do it at church, in Sunday school, or right at home!

READ TOGETHER

So many wonderful Bible storybooks are available that it can be difficult to choose! Look for one with simple language, short stories (to fit your child's attention span), and attention-getting art. If you're not sure which book is appropriate for your child, check the back cover. Many books will show the target age range.

> **Make a habit of praying together at regular times throughout the day.**

Here are a few you can try:

Little Blessings series (Tyndale House). In fun, whimsical rhyme, this series addresses questions from real kids on topics like "Who Is Jesus?" "Are Angels Real?" and "What Is Prayer?"
Uncle Andy's Bible Stories series (Baker Book House). Each story is followed by an easy activity. Your kids will have a great time dressing up like Elijah or creating edible mud!
Me Too! Series (Treasure Books). Each book shares

a Bible story and teaches children that while they may be little, they can do big things with God's help.

Parables Jesus Told and the Read Aloud Bible Stories series by Ella K. Lindvall (Moody).

The Rhyme Bible Storybook by L. J. Sattgast (Zondervan).

. . . 17 . . .

FAMOUS LAST WORDS[14]

A Positive Parent . . .

1. **Laughs easily.** Kids won't remember a spotless house; they will always remember the times when you dropped everything to laugh with them. I used to pretend I was writing a column on the funny things kids do and say, just to keep my sense of humor and sanity. (Tip: Write these things down right away!) Who would have dreamed these scribbled notes from a harried mother would end up as the foundation for a writing/speaking career?
2. **Blooms where she's budgeted.** When you have young kids and one of you is staying home—or

you're paying for some sort of child care—the money is usually *very* tight. This can be frustrating, sometimes even embarrassing. I drove an old station wagon (only the cool moms could drive minivans) for several years because it was cheap (as in "given to us") and held plenty of kids, their accompanying minnow buckets, fishing poles, assorted critters, and wet bathing suits. Be creative; have picnics in the park instead of going to McDonald's, make your own play dough, shop for resale bargains. Love, laughter, creativity, and your presence will cover up for the shortage of almost all material goods.

3. **Tries to find some way to say "I love you" every day.** You might forget to sign their homework papers. Perhaps you sent them to school with two different shoes on their feet. Maybe you gave them Frosted Flakes for dinner last night. But if you found a way to tell them you love them, much will be forgiven. Three magic phrases guaranteed to bring a grin: "I sure do love you, kiddo." "You are my sunshine—did you know that? You bring so much joy to my heart." "I'm so proud of you! Way to go!"

4. **Relaxes with her flaws.** Remember that the more you relax with your imperfections and theirs, the less the chance that you'll raise a little obsessive-

compulsive perfectionist. Teach them by modeling that there are some things you don't do very well, but you've learned to ask for help—and this gives other people the wonderful chance to feel needed!

For example, if you failed House-keeping 101, trade housecleaning with a Martha Stewart–type parent while you offer to baby-sit her kids, make dinner, or wallpaper her bath-room. God makes us all different for a reason: We need each other!

> Children teach us so much about God's love that we really can't experience any other way than by becoming a parent.

5. **Realizes her children are also here to teach her.** Here are a few things I've learned from children:

A king-size waterbed holds enough water to fill a 2,000-square-foot house 4 inches deep.

If you spray hair spray on dust bunnies and run over them with Rollerblades, they can ignite.

A three-year-old's voice is louder than two hundred adults in a crowded restaurant.

If you hook a dog leash over a ceiling fan, the motor isn't strong enough to rotate a forty-two-pound boy wearing Batman underwear and a Superman cape.

When you hear the toilet flush and the words "Uh-oh," it's already too late.

Play-Doh and *microwave* should never be used in
the same sentence.

The spin cycle on the washing machine doesn't
make earthworms dizzy, but it does make cats
dizzy; cats throw up twice their body weight
when dizzy.

We can learn how to have childlike dependence
from watching these little ones. What mother
hasn't secretly wished that she could be the one
who got to crawl up in someone else's lap to be
held and rocked and loved and soothed? Just as
our children reach for our hands in the dark, so
we parents—on our own individual dark days—
can always remember we're children of God. In
fact, Christ said that to enter his kingdom and
all he has for us, there's no other way to come
but to run into his arms, with the trust of a
small child. Children teach us so much about
God's love that we really can't experience any
other way than by becoming a parent. G. K.
Chesterton once said, "I've learned more about
God from observing children in nursery school
than from all the great theologians."

6. **Gathers a circle of support.** Perhaps the
preschooler years make up the time of life when
we most need other friends—particularly other

parents with kids the ages of our children. You can find them at MOPS groups at churches, Mom & Tot classes at the YMCA, or collapsed in exhaustion on small tables at fast-food-restaurant playgrounds. Put in the effort it takes to gather a group of three or four parents to meet on a weekly basis and share ideas, frustrations, prayers, and funny stories. You might, as a group, decide to trade baby-sitting nights one month, or bake double batches of freezable casseroles or goodies together while the kids play, or take the kids on a field trip to the zoo. Parents need other parents to keep from feeling isolated and overwhelmed. Again, I highly recommend mothers take advantage of Mom's Day Out programs. If your group of moms uses the same Mom's Day Out, you can go out together for lunch, to a movie, to get a makeover together, or to have a book-club afternoon.

7. **Gives her kids a hope-filled vision of the future.** Our kids desperately need for us to affirm a future filled with bright, purposeful, joy-filled lives. Assume that they will do well, and convey that God has created them to accomplish marvelous things. Have fun wondering and dreaming with them about what those things might be as they toddle, walk, and eventually fly from our parenting nests.

RESOURCES FOR PARENTS OF PRESCHOOLERS

FamilyLife Today: Publishes several quality Christian parenting resources. Visit them at www.fltoday.com

Focus on the Family: Provides tapes and books for almost every parenting dilemma. Call 1-800-A-Family to ask for information, or see their Web site: www.family.org

Hearts at Home: Dedicated to professionalizing motherhood. Includes conferences, resources, magazine. (www.heartsathome.org)

MOPS (Mothers of Preschoolers): Provides regular meetings with mothers in mind. Often includes child care, an inspirational speaker, a fun craft, time for sharing ideas, special events, and a radio program. See their Web site at www.mops.com

www.parentpwr.com: Sponsored by Brenda Nixon, this is an education source for parents of preschoolers. Nixon's book *Parenting Power in the Early Years* (Winepress) is a quick, easy read jam-packed with valuable information and a development chart.

BOOKS
Parent Picks
These are some of the books that are consistently getting the most rave reviews on-line from actual parents of preschoolers. Not surprisingly, there are some methods that work beautifully for some parents and children but fail miserably for others.

Again, we are all unique as parents and so are our

children. Find a method that you believe honors your spiritual values, your personality, and your child's temperament. Throw in a little common sense and some grace for imperfection, and enjoy! This time will pass all too fast.

1-2-3 Magic by Dr. Thomas Phelan (www.123magic.com). In both book and video form. Winner of the 1999 National Parenting Publisher Award.

How to Talk So Kids Will Listen by Adele Faber and Elaine Mazlish

Kid Cooperation: How to Stop Yelling, Nagging and Pleading to Get Kids to Cooperate by Elizabeth Pantley (intro by William Sears)

Kids, Parents and Power Struggles by Mary Sheedy Kurcinka

Parenting by Heart by Dr. Ron Taffel. Helps you understand how to connect with your kids in the face of too much advice, too many pressures, and never enough time.

Practical Parenting Tips: Over 1500 Helpful Hints for the First 5 Years by Vicki Lansky (Meadowbrook). Vicki has written over 25 books for parents and kids—easy to read, practical, down-to-earth.

Raising Your Spirited Child by Mary Sheedy Kurcinka

Rules for Parents: Simple Strategies that Help Little Kids Thrive and You Survive by Nan Silver

Sign With Your Baby by W. Joseph Garcia

Good General Reference Books
Caring for Your Baby and Young Child by the American Academy of Pediatrics

Complete Book of Baby and Child Care by Focus on the Family

. . .

Touch Points: Your Child's Emotional and Behavioral Development by Dr. T. Berry Brazelton

Books by Becky Freeman
Chocolate Chili Pepper Love

Coffee Cup Friendship and Cheesecake Fun

Peanut Butter Kisses and Mud Pie Hugs

Still Lickin' the Spoon

Worms in My Tea

For other titles and further resources, visit
www.beckyfreeman.com

Great Books for Kids
Alexander and the Terrible, Horrible, No Good, Very Bad Day
by Judith Viorst

Before I Dream by Karyn Henley

Bread and Jam for Frances by Russell Hoban

Chicka Chicka Boom Boom by John Archambault et al.

Curious George books

Good Night Moon by Margaret Wise Brown

Guess How Much I Love You by Sam McBratney

If You Give a Mouse a Cookie by Laura Joffe Numeroff

Ira Sleeps Over by Bernard Waber

King Bidgood's in the Bathtub by Audrey Wood

The Mitten by Jan Brett

Richard Scarry books

Runaway Bunny by Margaret Wise Brown

The Very Hungry Caterpillar by Eric Carle

Where the Wild Things Are by Maurice Sendak

· · ·

WEB SITES

www.athomemothers.com: colorful, informative magazine; great Web site to browse

www.childfun.com: rainy-day gold mine. Lots of creative activities and craft ideas for parent and child!

www.fathers.com: National Center for Fathering

www.foodfortots.com: ideas and recipes for feeding little ones

www.kidsource.com: provides a list of helpful, informative articles on all sorts of subjects and problems

www.practicalparenting.com: down-to-earth resources written parent to parent, by Vicki Lansky. Includes a free potty-training chart.

www.preksmarties.com: fairly commercial site, but interesting and educational. (And what parent doesn't think their pre-K child is a genius?)

www.preschoolerstoday.com: magazine style, lots of how-to and informational articles

www.webehave.com: fun, helpful products; advice for parents of special-needs kids

[1] Dr. James B. Maas, *Sleep Power* (New York: Villard Books, 1998), 134.
[2] Ibid., 59.
[3] Ibid., 65–66.
[4] Karen Scalf Linamen and Linda Holland, *Working Women, Workable Lives* (Wheaton, Ill.: Harold Shaw, 1983), 30.
[5] Susan M. Zitzman, *All-Day Care* (Wheaton, Ill.: Harold Shaw, 1990), 100–101.
[6] Lawrence Kutner, *Toddlers and Preschoolers* (New York: Avon Books, 1995), 21.
[7] Brenda Nixon, *Parenting Power in the Early Years* (Enumclaw, Wash.: WinePress Publishing, 2001), 43.
[8] Ibid., 43.
[9] Kutner, *Toddlers and Preschoolers,* 145.
[10] Nixon, *Parenting Power in the Early Years,* 39-40.
[11] Barbara Curtis, "Get Smart with Arts," *Today's Christian Woman,* May/June 2001, 30–33.
[12] Ross Campbell, M.D., *How to Really Love Your Child* (Wheaton, Ill.: Chariot Victor Books, 1977), 40.
[13] Ibid., 100–106.
[14] Reprinted from *Becoming Family,* 2001.

Marriage Alive International, Inc., founded by husband-wife team Claudia and David Arp, MSW, is a nonprofit marriage- and family-enrichment ministry dedicated to providing resources, seminars, and training to empower churches to help build better marriages and families. The Arps are marriage and family educators, popular speakers, award-winning authors, and frequent contributors to print and broadcast media. They have appeared as marriage experts on programs such as *Today, CBS This Morning,* and *Focus on the Family.* Their Marriage Alive seminar is in great demand across the U.S. and in Europe.

The Mission of Marriage Alive is to identify, train, and empower leaders who invest in others by building strong marriage and family relationships through the integration of biblical truth, contemporary research, practical application, and fun.

Our Resources and Services
- Marriage and family books and small-group resources
- Video-based educational programs including *10 Great Dates to Energize Your Marriage* and *Second Half of Marriage*
- Marriage, pre-marriage, and parenting seminars, including *Before You Say "I Do," Marriage Alive, Second Half of Marriage,* and *Empty Nesting*
- Coaching, mentoring, consulting, training, and leadership development

CONTACT MARRIAGE ALIVE INTERNATIONAL AT WWW.MARRIAGEALIVE.COM OR (888) 690-6667.

The Smalley Relationship Center, founded by Dr. Gary Smalley, offers many varied resources to help people strengthen their marriage and family relationships. The Center provides marriage enrichment products, conferences, training material, articles, and clinical services—all designed to make your most important relationships *successful* relationships.

The Mission of the Smalley Relationship Center is to increase marriage satisfaction and lower the divorce rate by providing a deeper level of care. We want to help couples build strong, successful, and satisfying marriages.

Resources and Services:
- Nationwide conferences: Love Is a Decision, Marriage for a Lifetime
- Counseling services: Couples Intensive program, phone counseling
- Video series, including *Keys to Loving Relationships, Homes of Honor,* and *Secrets to Lasting Love*
- Small group leadership guide
- Articles on marriage, parenting, and stepfamilies
- Smalley Counseling Center provides counseling, national intensives, and more for couples in crisis

CONTACT SMALLEY RELATIONSHIP CENTER AT WWW.SMALLEYONLINE.COM OR 1-800-84-TODAY.